# GATHERING THE ROLLING
# EXPERIENCES

## (A Collection of Management Case Studies)

BY

# D K Singhal & Dhawal Singhal

# GATHERING THE ROLLING EXPERIENCES
## (A Collection of Management Case Studies)

By

## D K Singhal & Dhawal Singhal

Copyright© D K Singhal & Dhawal Singhal 2016
Originally published in India

ISBN: 978-93-84314-71-2
Published by RIGI PUBLICATION

777, Street no.9, Krishna Nagar
Khanna-141401 (Punjab), India
Website: www.rigipublication.com
Email: info@rigipublication.com
Phone: +91-9357710014, +91-9465468291

# INDEX

# ACKNOWLEDGEMENT

Our special thanks are due to Mr. Mohit Singhal, CA, who proposed the idea of writing this book and guided time to time for presenting this book in present shape by his valuable suggestions.

August, 2016
D K Singhal
Dhawal Singhal

# PREFACE

We gather various experiences during work, during travelling, during vacations, during discussions with friends, and we learn a lot from these experiences if we really wish to do so. Some people learn from their own mistakes, while some learn from other's mistakes and experiences to ensure that problems are not able to hinder their path of success. For the second type of people, this book is an effort to present several case studies at one place from various sections of production- process, electrical, mechanical, management, administration etc.

All of the case studies presented here are real, directly or indirectly observed by any one of the authors; however, the names of persons have been changed due to obvious reasons.

# INTRODUCTION

Recently, I visited a well known university for presenting a guest lecture specially designed for third year mechanical students. There were more than 300 students attending the lecture. Before starting the lecture, I asked a simple question. "Someone has been assigned to bring a bearing number 6309 from the market. He calls you and asks about its size, because he wants to know if he can carry this bearing by hand, or need a tractor trolley or truck to bring it? Can you guide him?" Unfortunately, no hand rose. Everyone was silent. The last two digits in the bearing number, multiplied by five give the bearing bore. In this case, this is 09 X 5 or 45mm. If you know the bore of the bearing, you may, to a certain extent, easily guess about the bearing overall size or approximate weight. Our students study detailed technicalities of complex problems, but such small and simple problems often project a bad image of them.

I'd like to present another case, where a paper technologist, after completing his engineering degree joined a paper mill in south India. In the plant, he observed some huge brick shaped chemical was being added to a tank to get it dissolved in water before adding to pulp stock. He asked the operator the name of that chemical. The operator replied, "YELLAYUM". But, this man could not understand, so he repeated the question. The answer was the same. The student asked again. Annoyed with the repeated question, the operator spoke loudly, "YE-YELL-YOU-YAM, YELLAYUM". Now, he could understand that the chemical being added was ALUM, and he was unable to understand the name of chemical because of different accent of speaking there.

I don't know why but this story remained in my mind for a long time. Pronunciation of the word is another thing, but when a graduate needs to ask the name of such common additives, one must look back at our education system to check if we are over-focusing on books only.

The basic idea of the book is to present several case studies to think, update ourselves, and take necessary actions in order to get the best quality, best production, best profits, best customer satisfaction, best worker's interest in doing the job.

# Incandescent Bulb Vs. Tubelight

I took admission for Pulp & Paper Engineering at Institute of Paper Technology, University of Roorkee (now IIT, Roorkee) in 1986. In hostel, we were accommodated in double seated rooms. For lighting, there were two incandesce bulbs in each room. On talk with hostel supervisor, he told that university allocates more budgets for library, laboratories and other education related expenses.

We wrote an application to the director, asking for installation of tube lights in the hostel. In the application, we indicated potential energy savings and indicated about 'refund of money invested' in a couple of months. (Don't know why but, we could not even think of using the word 'payback' that time).

The director forwarded our application with a favorable note to the VC, who immediately called the director to meet personally the next day. We, the students, did not know what was going to happen.

On return, the director called me. With my heart beating fast (first time to meet the Director in his office, God knew if he was going to scold me or say something about the application), I went to the Director, who informed me that the VC was very pleased with the positive and logical approach by the students and immediately ordered installation of tube lights.

Around 30 years later, this may look as a small case, yet, gives a good food for thought. Presentation of your demands in a right way, with a positive approach results in better possibility of a favorable outcome.

# Approach towards Energy Audit

Several years back, I went to a mill for energy audit. In fact, the contract for energy audit was awarded to some other firm, but they had no experience of energy audit in a paper mill, so they needed my consultancy. On reaching I was stationed at a hotel in the city.

I had several known to in the mill, so the very first day, everything went on well. Department by department, we decided to move, taking observations and consolidate our findings after the initial round of the mill. One friend asked me the name of hotel where I was staying, which I told him.

In the evening, he came to hotel. Initially, we talked about several other friends, about family, life etc. After about an hour, I started becoming curious about his motive of coming to me. He was a resident of that city, and after a friendly talk, why he is not leaving. Anyhow, we took dinner and during this he asked me a favor, "*Jara hamara dhyaan rakhna!*" (Please do some favor for me while preparing the report.)

I was confused. What type of favor he is asking for? I asked him openly, what do you really want? And he explained in detail, "What are you going to do? You'll study the mill and suggest in place of this 22kW pump and motor on this pump, it should be of 15kW. But the management will not change the pump and motor immediately. There will be several meetings to decide whether to go for it or not. Finally, after around 6 months, these will be changed. But, after some time, when the equipment becomes weaker, we'll start facing problems due to smaller size of pump. For the same again meetings, discussions, postmortem, why the smaller size pump was installed and blah blah will continue. And, who is going to suffer? We! And we are responsible to maintain production. So please do not suggest anything for my department."

Later, his approach was visible in each department. The project department seemed to change every pump, every equipment, and every instrument. The purchase department wanted to buy everything from the cheapest supplier. The process men wanted nothing should be changed, if it is running well.

The result of approach was clearly visible. On paper machine wire part, to reduce electricity consumption, vacuum pumps were replaced with blowers. Project men were happy as the blowers were running well. Process men were happy as the vacuum pumps were running. Yes! They did not switch off the vacuum pumps, instead throttled the valves. So, in place of reducing electricity consumption, they actually increased it. In evaluation meetings, increased electricity consumption was justified for some improvement in quality and the chapter closed.

Always remember, to grow, a company needs to think with one brain. The first objective must be the synchronization of mindsets of all concerned with improvement.

# Purchasing a High Pressure Pump

You need some equipment, say pump. How do you normally proceed? Generate its indent, mention all details in it, and hand over the same to purchase department. Purchase department gathers enquiries from different suppliers, and sends back to project for technical approval. After approval, order is finalized after price negotiations considering various factors in mind, like customer list, reputation of supplier, delivery schedule etc.

Have you noticed one thing is certain? Before order finalization, the purchaser knows what does he need and the supplier knows what he is offering. Thus, mere the name of equipment is insignificant. Right? Read ahead.

A mill decided to install a DAF (Dissolved Air Flotation) cell, at effluent treatment plant. For the same, untreated effluent had to be pumped to DAF using a feed pump. A chemical dosing pump was also required. Also, a high pressure pump was needed to feed effluent through air dissolving tube where air will be mixed with effluent. The specifications of this pump were informed by the supplier as under-

High Pressure Pump
Head: 65M
Flow Rate: 40 KL/Hr.
Temperature: Ambient
Fluid: Water

While the requirement was passed on to some suppliers, they started sending their offers. However, a close friend indicated that I should not have used the word "High Pressure" in this case. Technically, only the pumps beyond 10 bar pressure (100 M head) are called as high pressure. For the mills DAF supplier even the 65

M head is too much, so he was calling it as high pressure pump. But, if I was giving full specifications indicating head and flow rate, does naming it as 'high pressure' make a difference?

Yes! It does. If you ask a supplier by that name, this pump will be costlier by 10-15%. He suggested creating a fresh enquiry to suppliers, without mentioning "High Pressure" in requirement. Finally, the offer price was lower by 10-12% for the same model of pumps. The discount was negotiated and the order was released.

While going to procure anything, always ask in such a way that you do not get overcharged.

# Testing of Starch

You are buying some chemical regularly for your process. Suddenly, a new supplier appears and offers you the same chemical at a much reduced price. What will you do? Ask for a sample for laboratory evaluation? Right?

Unfortunately, many consumers are not well equipped to test all the chemicals they are using. Many chemicals are supplied with the test reports, which however, have no relevance to the application of the chemical itself. You might have noticed the nature of some chemicals reported in the product specification sheet as non-ionic, while in the same sheet, the pH is reported as 7.0. (Just recall: pH is defined as the logarithm of hydrogen ion concentration.)

We faced this problem several years back. We were using starch and the grade used was "Amyloplast-10", being supplied by a reputed supplier. One day, another supplier, who was supplying several other chemicals to us, offered the same (under different brand name) but at much lower price. Instead of giving a sample, he offered to send one truck load of the material so that we may use it, and in case of any problem, he was ready that we can send all the material back to him. He had no datasheet/ specification sheet of the product. Freight was also going to be debited to his account.

This made the whole mill confused. Was the earlier supplier overcharging? Is there some defect in proposed chemical? Anyway, one truck of the starch was received the same week, but, was not used for several days. I discussed the case with a friend of mine, who is a Chartered Accountant. He asked me to whatsapp the invoice copy from both the suppliers to him. On sending the invoice copy, he replied *"Nahi Chalega"* (unsuitable).

Now this was too much. We are planning to send a sample of both the starches for testing in some reputed labs, and this man, without actual testing is denying the suitability of product, that too by studying the invoice only.

Later he told, "The grade of starch you have been using, had a column named "Excise" which is charged in invoice, but not the second one. Modified starches are excisable items, while raw starch is not. You had been procuring and using modified starches from the first supplier, but raw starch, which was sent to you by the second supplier, might be unsuitable for you, so I suggest you not to use it".

Later, an expert in the same field explained a short test method that could be used for testing of 'suitability' of starch in our lab. The test was done, and the results were same as indicated by the invoice.

If you are getting anything too cheap, ensure it is the same what you really need.

# Specific Water Consumption

You are making a product for which you need water. How do you report water consumption? Various units could use the production by weight, by number of products, per unit time etc. For a paper mill, the specific water consumption can be told as KL/T, KL/Day.

In the recent times, paper mills have taken a lot of steps to reduce water consumption. Over the past couple of decades, the specific water consumption (per ton of product) has reduced to just 10% or so, with many mills working towards ZLD (Zero Liquid Discharge).

I recall several years (around 12-15 years) back, a kraft paper mill indicated the problem of foul smell from paper as well as within the mill. The mill was using waste paper as raw material, and no such smell should arise by the process itself. They were facing the poor runnability of paper machine also due to excess fines (small pieces of papermaking fibers present in pulp). As an immediate solution, I suggested to drain a part of the backwater slightly for some time. But, that man just refused. He said, "My elder brother has allowed using only one tanker of water per day." It was a mill producing 25 ton paper per day, and working with one or two tanker (20KL) daily.

Then I asked him his specific water consumption, and got the unique answer. "Six Months". It was again a bigger surprise for me. Those days, water conservation was something we never took so seriously, but it was a new representation of specific water consumption. Failed to draw any conclusion, I asked again the meaning of "Six Months", and the reply was, "We fill all our storage chests, fresh water and back water tanks, reservoirs etc with fresh water, run our plant for six months, and after that drain all the remaining water in tanks etc.; fill in fresh water, and restart the plant again. One or two tankers per day help us in maintaining the water loss due to evaporation during paper making."

Needless to say, this small meeting changed my approach towards water consumption. We are now working hard for water conservation, but achieving a target of "Six Months" looks a distant dream, at least for the grades of paper we manufacture.

We all need and use benchmarks. However, with time, even the benchmarks need to be upgraded.

# Weak Roll or Weaker Decisions

This is a case of a large scale paper mill. The paper maker called me one day that they were facing problem at pope reel. Pope reel is the end of paper machine, where paper is rolled on a rotating tambour roll with the friction of a roll named as pope drum. To hold the tambour roll against pope drum, load is applied through pneumatic or hydraulic cylinders. The design is such that there should not be any wrinkle or crease while the paper gets wrapped on the tambour roll.

But for past several months, the mill was facing problem of friction marks, crease, wrinkle etc, at the beginning of the roll. After some time, when the roll diameter increased the paper was without any defect. We discussed a lot of options to solve the problem. Unfortunately, being associated to that mill, he was not allowed to email me or officially to discuss the issue with me. So, almost every fortnight or so, we discussed in a friendly way. After a few discussions, we began to believe that there was something wrong with the rolls. I asked him to take a nip impression by putting a plain paper backed with carbon paper between two rolls, to see if there is any deflection in any of the roll, and this revealed the origin of the problem. Over time, the tambour rolls became too week and due to bending of rolls, the paper was getting damaged. The solution now seemed very simple. Replace tambour rolls.

Again 3-4 months passed. We both were busy, and no phone calls. So I decided to call him to know the status. But the problem was exactly the same as it was earlier. He informed the management has hired some big consultant who has suggested an upgrade of the complete pope reel, and the price negotiations are on. They have proposed an upgrade of pope reel section with around 20-40 million rupees. The replacement of pope reel, after finalization of order will take around 4-6 months. I said, "Why did you not raise a question of just replacing the tambour roll? Each of the 10-12 rolls may cost around 50-80 thousand or so. If you wish, you may order a roll and get it ready within 10 days from any good reputed Indian supplier." Then I asked, had he quantified the losses? He had, and the losses were to the tune of 3-5 ton paper per day. That means the cost of one tambour roll costs less than the cost of production loss for just two days.

A few days later, he informed me that the mill had finalized the order for the replacement of pope reel including the tambour rolls for nearly 40 million rupees. The replacement may require a downtime of 3-4 days also.

Nearly three months have passed as on today while I am writing about the event. In these three months, I am unable to decide, "Which is weaker- The tambour roll or the managements decision?"

The aim here was not to challenge the management for its decisions. The management might have taken this decision considering some more issues with the machine. Still, I strongly believe, those directly and deeply involved with the process, must be explained about the new decision.

# DG Overtime Issue

When the plant was started, the cost of HSD was less and hence electricity generated from a DG set was cheaper than that purchased from state electricity boards. So, it was decided to continue production with electricity from DG sets and the decision for getting an electricity connection from state electricity board was postponed.

Due to shortage of DG operators, the helpers were trained and we continued with them. Over a year or so, no DG operator applied. Meanwhile, the helpers were promoted as assistant operators, and they began to understand things. Our formula was simple. They knew how to start and stop DG set, and in case of any abnormality, they had to just shut the DG set, start the standby one, and to inform the management.

With time, some of them started leaving the mills due to getting better opportunities or other personal reasons. This is a routine feature that if you train a worker to perform better, he gets better opportunities with other mills. Suddenly, two operators fell sick – Jaundice. We knew they won't be able to resume for a month or so. Now, we had five operators only. We made an action plan. Two operators will be there in a shift. Each one will work 12 hours a day, with fifth day as weekly off. In place of a regular shift of 8 hours, for extra four hours, overtime shall be given. In addition, in place of four weekly offs, they get 6 offs.

However, the next morning the DG in-charge approached with all the five operators and their joint resignation with immediate effect. They were not ready to do overtime. To get some time to act upon, I just asked them to write separate resignations and come to office. Meanwhile, I asked DG in-charge not to feel tense. I said that both he and I were capable of working as operators. We'll hire more helpers, he'll do day shift and I'll do night shift, both of us would train the new helpers and within some time, everything was normal. He felt a little assured.

Few minutes later, one operator came to my office with his resignation letter in hand. I asked him, why he was not interested in revised schedule? He said, 12 hours shift means that extra work after 12$^{th}$ hour will be considered for overtime. I explained him the whole situation indicating that extra work after 8 hours shall be considered for overtime, and in addition, you would get more weekly offs with the new, but temporary system and he was convinced. The same thing went well with three more operators. Then the fifth operator appeared.

The fifth operator was not at all ready to do overtime. Why? The mill had been in bad finances, and overtime of past 4 months was pending. I asked him about his pending overtime which was nearly Rs. 230 or so. Then, I asked how much increment did he get during last pay? The answer was Rs. 800 over Rs. 3200 as previous salary. Now, it was seemingly much easy to explain him. Mill had poor finances, but as the condition improved, it considered the priority as to increase salaries first. That decision of salary increase was made in April. As the salaries of January were not given by that time, it was decided to pay increased salary effective January itself. The mill could have simply declare that the increased salaries will be considered from the month of April onwards, and rather clear the overtime pending, but the mill chose a tougher but employee friendly route.

Even after the discussions, he felt that the overtime was not being given in time so working for overtime was something not good for him. Secondly, for a small overtime of say Rs. 230 (what he earned during past few months), he will have to do an overtime of 4 hours a day for the whole month in future. Explaining everything to him was a difficult time, and I had to spend more than an hour for it. Still, he took a couple of days, before finally coming to me and saying that now he was convinced we did the right thing. Needless to say he was the person who initiated the group resignation.

# MG Plate Procurement

This took place in 2004. We needed to replace our existing drying cylinder (MG Cylinder) of the paper machine with a new one. For uniform heat transfer, as well as for good life, the shell of the cylinder must be made of defect free steel. The order was placed to a supplier, and after he informed that the plate has been reached at his site, I along with a UT (ultrasound tester) approached him for plate checking. The dimensions of the plate were around 8500mm X 3200mm X 65mm.

The standard method for UT analysis includes making a grid pattern having 9" X 9" by chalk. Now each and every square block has to be checked thoroughly. The testing person proceeded to do so. Then suddenly, a worker said, "Don't do like this. Spread your hands and wave the probe at larger distance." I asked, "Why". His innocent replay was, "If you do this, the plate will not get rejected." Obviously, our aim was to identify any defect, and approve only the defect free plate. Well, there were flaws and hence the plate got rejected.

Over the next 3-4 days, we visited many workshops, many steel traders locally, but the suitable size and UT OK plate was not available. So, the supplier suggested that we should consider using imported plate. It is available at Kalamboli (Near Mumbai), but at a higher price. It must be noted that Kalamboli is the biggest steel market in south Asia. The only condition was that we were allowed to do the testing there only and after approval, we shall have MG cylinder from this plate only. Once accepted, the supplier will not take the plate back. We accepted for this.

Now we had a doubt. If the plate is OK, and after testing we approve it, and in place of lifting this plate, the supplier procures some other plate how can we know? Taking an ultrasound tester every time from Delhi to Ahmedabad / Kalamboli is not that easy. We thought of marking the plates with punch, but similar punch marks can be made easily. After all, they were running good workshops.

I took a small pack of white paint. After testing, when we were sure that that plate was OK, I spilled a little paint from a height of around one meter on to the plate. The paint dried after a few minutes, and I took photographs of this plate using a digital camera. One can understand it is extremely difficult to produce the same pattern on another set of plates. After the plates reached Ahmedabad at the workshop, I could easily tell that the plates have not been replaced.

# Worker Sleeping at Night

Night shift is generally a difficult one, as one may feel sleepy while on duty.  Almost every management faces problems due to workers sleeping on duty, and some case may become extremely dangerous or hazardous. Some workers want to work, but sleep unintentionally, while some consider this (night) shift as a boon to complete their sleep.

I recall in a paper mill, the worker went to paper machine area, took many big sheets of paper; went to central laboratory located around 500 meters away, removed some empty drums and placed the sheets behind these to prepare his bed, folded some more paper and prepared a pillow, and slept. On being caught red handed by the checking staff, he said, "I just felt a little sleepy."

Several mills have developed some unique ways to avoid such situations. Some mills impose penalty of half to one day of salary, some mark it in employee register and consider it as a negative point while considering salary hikes. Here, I am going to share some practices been followed in different paper mills.

Mill A identified some good workers, who did not sleep and took their duties seriously. Later the responsibility of whole shift not sleeping was given to them. They jointly made a small group and it was decided if a worker is found sleeping, his shoes / chappals are collected by the team and hidden at a safe place. If the event gets repeated, do the same thing again. After he did it several times, all five or six pairs of shoes are kept near him. Obviously, he would like to take all the shoes with them. But, now the security guards will stop him at the main gate, and ask him to stand on the main gate (worker gate) for an hour or so with all shoes in his hands. This way all workers know that he had been sleeping regularly while on duty. Within 6 months, the scheme got a hit, and worker sleeping problem reduced to a minimum.

In another mill; say Mill B, the workers started putting old grease on both sides of a sleeping worker. If the worker turns while sleeping, his clothes got dirty. One may understand how difficult it to remove grease stains from the clothes is. To a certain extent, this also worked well.

In a typical case, a mill decided to immediately fire the sleeping worker, paying his all salary and dues the next day. An interesting case happened. As a worker needs to give a notice for a month or so before leaving the job, otherwise, his 30 days salary may be deducted; a worker decided to sleep in night shift. Before going to sleep, he instructed another worker "I am going to sleep. After 10 minutes, you inform security that I was sleeping so that they may be able to catch me red handed." The next day, all his dues were cleared all payments made, and he was relieved from the job. On getting full payments, he smiled and said, "I got another job, and found this a better way to leave a company." Later, the mill converted its approach to a conventional one. Security staff too periodical round in the plant, and anyone found sleeping was informed to the management in the morning, who took actions like marking half a day absent or so.

I must share a case while a DG operator started filling HSD in DG service tank. The mill had three DG sets each of 380kVA, with service tanks of 990 liter capacity each. Every shift, the operator had to transfer HSD from storage tank to service tanks in order to keep DG sets running continuously. To maintain records, initial and final level of DG set service tank was noted, and estimated consumption during filling time was added to this to obtain actual HSD supplied to DG set. This DG operator started the transfer pump, and as filling the service tanks would need 6-8 minutes, sat on chair and got asleep. The service tank overflew, and when he woke up, he tried to cover the negligence. He put a lot of sand over spillage, cleaned the area thoroughly, thinking nobody will be able to detect it.

Next morning, while going through the reports, I found some mismatch. The storage tank and service tank figures showed around 250-300 liters of HSD difference. I visited the DG sets, service tanks, and found indication of what might had happened at night. I sent one person to call the operator and his assistant both. After a short discussion, he admitted that he got slept while filling the service tank and his assistant had gone to toilet that time, so some HSD spillage took place.

Now, the challenge was to take action against him. The loss was around Rs. 4000-4500 (at that time cost of HSD was around Rs. 15.00-16.00 per liter), and he was unable to pay such a huge amount. So, I informed him that due to his negligence, the mill has incurred a loss of nearly Rs. 4000, and he would have to compensate for the losses. I further informed him to see me tomorrow and then I'll decide what action had to be taken against him.

I knew for him paying this money was not possible. So next day, I offered him four possibilities-

1. Company has incurred a loss of Rs. 4000-4500, so you decide an adequate cash penalty yourself. You are a part of company, and I trust you; so whatever amount you decide, I'll accept your decision.
2. Take a small board, write on it that "Due to my sleeping at night, mill faced a loss of more than 250 liters of diesel" and with a security guard, go and show this board to at least 50 workers in the mill.

3. Get some sweets (I'll pay the money for it), distribute to at least 50 workers and whoever asks the reason, tell him, "I want to feel sorry for more than 250 liters of diesel spilled due to sleeping at night."
4. If you have some better punishment option for you, you tell me.

Well, he was unable to tell me immediately, so I allowed him to think and decide in a day. Next day, again he came to me and expressed that he was unable to decide. Again, he was asked to think and decide by next day. This went for three days. The fourth day, I told him that I was not going to take any action for that incident, and he should concentrate to his work.

Well, three days of punishment of 'the fear of unknown punishment' was enough for him. Needless to say, afterwards, I never heard that he slept or even showed laziness on duty.

Worker sleeping at night could be dangerous for himself, for his colleagues as well as for the mills itself. No definite method works always all the time. You need to explore and implement different methods time to time.

# Boiler Chemical

Maintaining proper conditions of boiler water is the key to get the best results in terms of boiler efficiency and life. Initially, while installing the boiler, I read the manual two-three times, and noted all the relevant points related to its operation. Initially, for the makeup feed water, softener was installed as the fresh water quality in the area was really good. A few months later, when the boiler in-charge left the mills and another one joined, he demanded some boiler additive should be used in boiler. By that time, we had not been using any chemical for boiler. I talked to some of my friends, some chemical engineers, and decided to procure TSP (Tri Sodium Phosphate). TSP acts as sludge conditioner and anti scalent. It increases pH also. The cost of TSP that time was nearly Rs. 25 per kg. Instead, I asked the boiler in-charge that I have procured a chemical from a big company, and the cost is Rs. 250 per kg. It was to be added at a dose of 250 gm per shift in boiler feed water tank.

Within a couple of hours, when I reached Boiler, during my routine round, he came to me- overjoyed, "Now the boiler is running very well. This chemical is really good." I checked all parameters but could not find any difference in any of the parameter compared to few hours earlier. So, I asked him, "What difference, actually, do you see? All parameters are same as they were earlier." But he said, "Parameters are important at their own position, but now it feels that the boiler is running better."

I understood, there was no use of debating with him. To me it was just a matter of less than a cost of Rs.500-600 per month. In the next few months many boiler chemical suppliers came, almost each supplying chemical to nearby mills. They offered frequent testing of boiler water, feed water and assuring that the boiler tube life will increase after the use of chemical suggested by them. In fact, I tried a few chemicals but find no difference in boiler performance so discontinued.

As the time passed, I began to realize that for a low pressure boiler, these chemicals are just useless. Then one smart chemical supplier appeared. He gave a good powerpoint presentation on his laptop, showed how the boiler tubes get choked with scaling, thus resulting in loss of boiler efficiency; how the tubes corrode in absence of correct pH; and how little is the cost of his chemical compared to boiler replacement due to these problems. After he finished his presentation, I asked him several questions-

1. As per boiler supplier boiler water TDS should be less than 3500. I have informed my operators that I want it to be less than 3000. They are getting blow down TDS of around 2500. As during sampling, some of the water gets evaporated, in fact inside boiler, the actual TDS level is around 2200-2300 or so. Why should I use a sludge conditioner in such a case?

2. I test boiler blow down daily, and the pH is within specified limits. Why should I use a pH booster?

3. My condensate return is more than 80%, and feed water temperature exceeds 85°C. At this high temperature, there is practically no dissolved oxygen in water. Why should I use oxygen scavenger in this case?

4. Apart from all above three points, how the chemical you are suggesting, is going to help me?

Obviously, he had no answer to any question so he left assuring to come back soon with his GM who had good technical knowledge. He did not come back again. We continued without any chemical. After 10-12 years of operation, our boiler tube got punctured. This followed by another two tubes within next three months, then another three after two months. So we decided to go for another boiler.

As the new boiler was being installed, suppliers started visiting again. But now, I was filled with confidence. We decided to install an RO (Reverse Osmosis) plant almost immediately after the new boiler was installed. Again a supplier approached, and I asked him several questions-

1.  Tell me the name of any mill, where chemical supplied by you is running for past 5 years.

2.  This mill should assure that there had been no boiler tube leakage during past five years.

3.  This mill should confirm that they do not need de-scaling after using chemical supplied by you. And, finally-

4.  This mill must assure that during past five years, it has NOT tried any other boiler chemical. (If a mill is fully satisfied with your product, why it is trying other chemicals?)

He seemed very confident for first question, seemed confident after second and third question, but after hearing the fourth question, he asked me time to get the answer of the same and come back again. Needless to say, he did not return back.

Things went well for a few years. Later a friend of mine installed a new boiler and a small turbine (3MW) in his plant. He is a reputed calcium carbonate manufacturer. After some time of operation, there was some problem with the turbine, and the turbine supplier was called to visit the site. On inspection, he informed that the steam contains some solids, indicating that the boiler water was contaminated. RO plant was running well, and its properties were OK. To cross check, I asked him to send a sample of RO water to me, but it was perfect for his application.

He faced the same problem several times. After three months, he recalled that he was adding some chemical to boiler. Could the chemical be creating problems? On investigation, the results were positive. Immediately, he discontinued using boiler chemical and then after, he has not faced even a single problem due to contamination with steam in his turbine.

The same thing works for other applications too. We, keep on investing in different items/products just for additional benefits, and discontinue only after some problem associated appears.

# DCS System

Long back I was working for a big mill. The mill had two paper machines and the third was going to be installed. On joining I was placed in Paper Machine department, and things went on smoothly for some time. One of the paper machine had a DCS-QCS (Distributed Control System-Quality Control System) installed, with a computer with a touch screen. Those days, computers were rare to find, and touch screen was something like miracle for most. DCS had three modes- Operator, Supervisor and Engineer. Operator mode was for most routine operations, changing quality etc. Machine speed, steam pressure and other parameters will automatically set by the computer as per given set of parameters. In supervisor mode, set-points for different quality of paper, raw material mix etc. could be programmed. In engineering mode, you can virtually write the program, modify all settings etc. The default mode was operator. Well, as it uses a computer, there was an AC cabin, and going inside the cabin for a few minutes was something great. Being a newcomer, we were not allowed to go into DCS cabin.

The system was supplied by Tata-Honeywell, one of the most reputed supplier in this area; and being with my educational background with a little knowledge of control systems, PID controllers, instrumentation etc., I soon made a friendship with Tata-Honeywell engineers. We discussed about the system, and within some time, I was able to understand the functionalities of the system. I soon observed that the operators (including the paper makers and chief paper maker) used to put the system in 'manual' mode, made quality changes as required, and later on put it in 'auto' mode. I started working on it, and found a little 'bug' in the system. I requested the engineers on personal ground that they should disable the function for a couple of days temporarily, which they agreed after getting convinced with my justification. Next day was Sunday, and I decided to change quality in 'auto' mode only. The response was good. Hardly 12 minutes of paper was slightly off quality. I took a printout of the results.

Next day, I showed the chart to my boss, paper maker. He became annoyed. "Who will justify the 12 minutes of paper lost by this computer?" Now, I showed him another chart indicating more than 25 minutes of off grade paper produced while he, himself changed quality in manual mode. I said, "Sir, a couple of days back, you made quality change in manual mode, there was 40 minutes off quality paper, out of which 25 minutes production was totally unusable while in this case, off quality is just a little deviating from standards. With a little adjustment in the computer algorithm in the engineer mode, this system can be tuned to reduce these 12 minutes to 3-4 minutes." He took both the charts from me and went to his office, without uttering a single word. My heart was beating, as I was thinking, "Had I not preserved the chart of earlier condition with 40 minutes off quality production, my image had been lost."

After a few minutes, he called me in his office, and asked, "What do you want?" "Sir, I want to modify the control logic after the size press, so that there is no production loss at all. By that, that 12 minutes loss can be reduced to 3-4 minutes only." He seemed convinced. However, convincing Chief Paper Maker, DGM was difficult, and finally they allowed the change in control logic.

I got a lesson from this- "If you are going to project your achievements to someone, always be prepared as the other one may prove the same as your failure."

# Labor Supervision

Later on, I was shifted to project department. A new paper machine was going to be installed- biggest and fastest in north India, that time. I and one of my colleagues, Vishal reported to project department next day. Everyone was congratulating. For us, it was just a department change. But, soon, we came to know that many people were trying to get recommendations of seniors and other influencing people to get into project department. Working with that machine was dream for many.

The initial assignment was a simple one. For machine shed, a big hall 180 meter long and 36 meter wide had to be prepared, but the ground level was high. So, the land had to be excavated by 600-650mm. For the same, there were 25-30 laborers doing the work manually under a supervisor. No JCB or such machines were being used that time. Guess, what was our job? Yes, our job was to supervise this team!

Within a couple of days, we started feeling sad. Have we done engineering to supervise this? Anyhow, we requested management that as we are supervising the job, there is no need of any other supervisor. He may be deputed with some other work. Next day we were also deputed in shifts. One to report in general (day) shift, while another in B (2:00PM to 10:00PM) shift, shifts rotating every week.

Here I took another action. While I had been in General shift, I asked one of the workers to take a broom, and clean the area. Furthermore, if some other worker wants to go to drink water or for a short break, this person had to be asked instead of asking me; well under my direction to allow only one person at a time or so. In this way, I was developing a supervisor. But, that supervisor too was not permanent. Out of remaining workers, whoever was found working harder was to be awarded this responsibility for next three days. May we call the system as "supervisor by rotation". To be a supervisor for next three days, the other workers started working hard, and the whole team efforts were apparently visible to the seniors.

Very soon, the seniors noticed that if I was in morning shift, the plant looked very neat and clean. Furthermore, the excavation output was more in my presence. When the machine supply started, I was given the responsibility of a section independently, while Vishal worked under someone.

Whenever I recall the time and efforts done that way, I came to the conclusion, "Do whatever job has been assigned to you with full capability and full efficiency and try to incorporate the new ideas for its improvement. Your work may get unnoticed for a long time, but sooner or later, you will definitely get the results."

# Speeding Up of the Project

For installation of plant, you need pipeline, pipe fittings etc. As it was a big project, the requirement was also big. For the same, the project manager made a decision. We decided to note down each and every pipeline, prepare BOM (Bill of Material) for each pipeline separately. This was consolidated for each section of the plant, and final total gave complete requirement. The strict instruction was to calculate the requirement as exactly as possible. No factor of safety to be added. Well, the consolidated requirement was prepared and sent to GM for approval. He reduced the quantity by nearly 5% saying that they had a lot of scrap pipelines in the scrap yard. Later, Vice President again reduced by 5% on the same reason. When the final requirement was sent to head office, they further reduced the requirement by 10% and orders were placed. This was going to create problems, but probably the lack of communication between project department and authorities was the real culprit.

This was September and work was going on normally. Shed and foundations were being ready, no arrival of any machine or equipment was being seen or expected within that week. Suddenly, all involved were called for an urgent meeting. We had no idea about the objective of meeting. Then the VP arrived. He made just a small statement- "Arrangement of a computer and a computer operator has been made in the small room near project office. Anybody involved with the project department can go there, get his bio data typed, printed. Send to any number of mills or employers you wish to. All stationery, printing and postage expanses shall be borne by the company. But, in case you are unable to reel the paper on this machine by 31$^{st}$ of March, nobody involved with the project will be allowed to continue his job on 1$^{st}$ of April. Thank you." He left then.

Needless to say, we all got determined to do our bit at any cost to save our jobs, but did not know that the inventory was going to become a villain.

The next day was not normal. Everyone knew that if something has to be done, it must be done. No excuse can work if the project gets delayed. By the noon, we got intimation that the project manager is going to take a meeting. In the meeting, all charts were prepared, schedules and targets were assigned. I was assigned the job of 'approach flow' section to be installed with a capital cost of approx. Rs. 180 million. It was further decided that a daily progress review meeting shall be held at 5:00 PM at site office.

I made details about my section, and divided the whole job in different sections. I prepared a list of all pumps, pipelines, equipment etc. so that the monitoring can be done in a proper way. On the basis of it, I approached to contractor but came to know, that he was not doing that job. The management had assigned different type of jobs to different contractors –there were seven contractors working for my section- who further assigned the jobs to their petty contractors. Thus there were a team of 35 petty contractors working for the project. And we did not know who will do what kind and type of job. Soon, I came to know that I have to deal with nearly 10-11 contractors.

I tried to approach project office to get information about who will do jobs related to my areas, but, could not get any information. So, I approached to contractors. I discussed with one of them, and soon came to know about some part which could be done by him. So I asked him the schedule for work for the next three-four days. Next, I asked him, if he had all the required material available for completing the job. Most of the material was with him, only a few pipelines, short bends, and collars were required. I left, and went to store, located the items, prepared a stores requirement slip and started searching for my boss, who can sign the slip for getting the material. I found him after nearly an hour, got the slip signed and handed over to contractor.

This was something new for the contractor. Earlier, he used to run behind the project staff to get the material and requirement slip signed. In return, he gave me reward by speeding up the work I was looking into. Deadline was approaching nearer, and the work was in full throttle. By the end of January, the problem due to pipelines etc. started appearing. Equipments are installed, pumps are installed, motors have been mounted, electrical have been set right, but, the stock needs a pipeline to move from pump to the concerned equipment. I started looking for old pipelines- which were usable, which were in good condition, which were lying ignored in the scrap yard. Every evening I went to contractors, their petty contractors and asked for the expected material requirement for next couple of days. The next morning, I visited scrap yard, located the usable material, went to the contractors offices; tell them from where the material is available.

If you have assigned any order to a contractor, the contractor earns more if he gets all the materials, permissions etc. in time, and becomes able to finish his job faster. Simultaneously, you find it easier to meet your deadlines easily for no additional investment or expenditure.

# Pipeline Theft

Around 4 days prior to deadline, except one railing pipe, everything was finished. But that particular pipeline, a 40mm NB was not available anywhere. Now, the supervisor of a petty contractor came to me and offered a 'solution', "Sir, I have got information that 40mm new pipeline have been unloaded in the boiler house today, but those are all IBR[*] approved. We need only one piece of it. Tonight, if you accompany us, I along with one of my welder can go there and bring one pipeline. Tonight is a dark night and moon will not appear in the sky. Nobody will be able to catch us. During night, I'd wipe off the IBR mark using a grinder, and by morning you will see the pipeline in its place, well painted so that nobody could be able to identify about it." The boiler house was nearly one and a half kilometer away from our project site.

For a moment, I got stunned. It was just a theft. We are going to complete the erection of a new paper machine with pipeline stolen from boiler house that too an IBR pipe for railing purpose. That grade of pipe costs around 10-20 times more compared to conventional railing pipe. Anyway, I nodded. My section was going to get ready for commissioning three days prior to deadline.

Later just on the day of commissioning, when I told my project manager about it, he started shouting on me-, "You used a stolen pipeline for this? Singhal, you are......." But with each word, his volume reduced and his eyes opened up more and more. After all, he was going to get credit for completing the assignment in time.

** IBR stands for "Indian Boiler Regulation". IBR approved pipelines are thicker and heavier and typically 10-20 times costlier than conventional pipelines.*

# Sheet Cutter Gear Safety

Paper is made in form of rolls, from which smaller reels are cut. Small sheet cutters were installed for cutting these small reels to sheets. The sheet cutters were of very old design, and to get the desired size of sheet (sheet width shall remain the same as per the parent reel width) the operators needed to change the gears. As there might be any sheet size requirement, so a huge number of gears were piled near the sheet cutter.

Occasionally, the operators mounted a particular set of gear, check the length of paper being cut and decide if a slightly bigger or smaller gear is needed. The earlier set was removed and replaced with another set, to check if paper length is adequate or not. If it is adequate, continue with the sheet production. However, if you are going to mount gears for checking, you know you will run the machine only for a few minutes, check the paper length, and stop the machine in case the length is improper. This creates a temptation to not mount the safety guard over the gear-set. As a result, many a times, the operators forgot and it started becoming a habit that the machine may be run without safety guards in place. Frequent warnings did not give satisfactory results. Meanwhile a couple of minor accidents took place–only scratches on skin-, we started repeated ordering to operators, they followed the instructions; but next time, they might forget again.

In fact, an accident is never minor. It is just a big warning towards a bigger accident if you fail to mend your ways. We knew some major accident was going to take place. But we are unable to find a way to save ourselves. Then suddenly an idea appeared.

Immediately, we decided to impose a cash fine of Rs. 50 against the operator in which presence the cutter is found running without guards in place. Most companies hesitate in such deductions as they do not like to 'earn' from workers salary. So, the question again was, "what to do with such Rs. 50?" The electrical In-charge suggested a good approach, "tea and sweets/snacks etc. may be distributed to shift helpers and other workers in the sheet cutter area". The results were enlightening. The problem of sheet cutter operation without guards got almost solved. Finally, the bigger accident, which was almost sure to take place, had to mend its way.

This continued for few months. Finally, the operators started getting used to of running sheet cutters ONLY if the safety guards are in place. Later, we replaced those old cutters with new cutters based on PIV gear box.

# Consistency Transmitter Malfunction

We install various instruments in process to timely and accurately monitor and control the process. In a newly installed paper mill world class instrumentation and control system was installed. There was a complete DCS/QCS system, more than 3000 sensors to monitor process and parameters related to the quality of paper. Out of these, there was one 'consistency transmitter'.

For those having no background of paper mill operations, I must indicate the process briefly. Pulp going to paper machine was being monitored by a consistency transmitter (for measurement of pulp concentration or consistency) and magnetic flow meter (for measurement of flow rate). The multiplication of these two figures gives dry stock flow rate, which is controlled so that the paper made has a constant basis weight (gsm, grams weight of paper per square meter of area, an important paper property). To further control the system, there was an on-line scanner, which measured the basis weight of paper (gsm), and in case of any deviation, controlled the set point of dry stock flow rate, which was done by altering the set points of consistency and stock flow rate.

In case there is some problem in paper machine, like dryer electrical tripping, or paper breaking and getting jammed in the machine, the pulp stock feed pump was stopped. After a short while, when the pump started, the control system malfunctioned and gsm fluctuated in the range to 40 to 80 against the desired 60gsm. Within a short time, the control system maintained the desired value of 60+2 gsm, but the production during this time has to be rejected due to being off-quality.

One of my colleagues came out with a unique solution. Whenever you want to stop stock pump for a short while, put the whole system in manual mode; and when you start the pump again, wait for the process to stabilize for 5-10 minutes, and if everything is OK, put the whole system in AUTO again. This was a great idea. There was no off-quality production. Slowly and slowly, habit started developing to run the system in manual mode. Everyone was happy, except the instrumentation men and QCS supplier engineers. They tried to discuss with many process people one by one but everyone shrugged, "We need to run the plant with acceptable quality product only." Later they approached me. My words were almost the same. However, I was able to explain them the problem in detail, indicating that the transmitter works too slow for my process.

My words hit the QCS engineers hard, and they lost control. Instrumentation people were also with them, and I was alone. They challenged, "Mr. Singhal! You are not living in 23rd century. This is just 21$^{st}$ century. And, this is the fastest transmitter available in the world." After some time, the project manager called me. Without asking any explanation or anything, he said, "Singhal! Why do you want to create problems? Let the system run as it is. Don't talk to them." I needed to do something. I explained him it was the software problem, and I could solve it if I get just a couple of hours with QCS engineer, Mr. Nelson. But that will need a change in the computer program written by them.

Today, it seems just a small issue, but consider the time of mid nineties, where computers were not so common. Most people looked these as something very critical. Anyway, I must thank project manager Mr. Goswami, who, did not know well about how that could be done, but trusted me, and convinced the management for a change in control logic. Now, it was my turn to convince Mr. Nelson. For him, I was just a paper technologist, with a little knowledge about computers, who was telling him that his program needs a change- "His Program". Anyway, we discussed for some time, and I explained him the problem.

"The consistency transmitter was something like a mixer fitted in pipeline, and depending upon the pulp consistency (concentration), the force to rotate its impeller is a function of stock consistency. But, when the pump is stopped, for some time, the pulp returns back to the chest and thus the sensor head keeps on sensing consistency. The sensed value differs significantly from the previous one only after some time, as the pulp flow stops after some time. The last value observed by the transmitter is saved in the systems memory and when the pump is started again, the setting is made according to the new value, thus resulting fluctuations."

The solution we both worked was to freeze the consistency set point value automatically when the pump is stopped. This way, there should not be any problem when the pump is started again, and operator can put it back to auto mode. He took just half an hour to include is 'subroutine', and thereafter the problem was finished.

There were many paper making experts, but I was, somehow able to explain Mr. Nelson about the problem and possible solution because of a little knowledge from both the fields. Otherwise, the process engineers had accepted to operate that section in manual mode.

This incidence looks a purely technical issue, but, this gives a strong need to develop communication between the developer (who is generally an IT expert) and the user (who is generally the process engineer). In case the user is not able to explain his problems in a language the IT expert can understand or vice versa, the targets will always be difficult to achieve.

# Paper Production Loss Monitoring

What is the difference between the mindset of an operator and a manager? Often the operator is concerned with the production only, and the manager wants each and every piece of information along with the production and quality. The information so gathered is then used to further enhance the production, productivity, quality, cost competitiveness etc.

In a small paper mill, management started a new approach. Instead of having focus on production, they started focusing on downtime and joints in paper. Paper making being a continuous operation, if there is a break (joint) in paper web during manufacturing, the restoration work needs nearly 2-5 minutes. Most downtime are either from mechanical or electrical side, so it was decided to deal with the problem of electrical and mechanical issues separately, and only the process part shall be taken up separately. If there is a joint, that must be reported.

Many paper consumers want paper to be supplied to them in reel form. If there is a joint in the reel, they may face production problems, so number of joints per reel becomes an important parameter. So, some operators started a practice that in case of a web break while the roll is going to be almost ready, they just changed the roll. This way, that joint does not appear to have occurred. For the quality point that was OK, but, for process monitoring, it was a bad practice. So, it was decided to install a paper break detector on the machine.

The concept of the paper break detector is very simple. There is a light source and a detector aligned properly. In case of normal operation, paper hinders the path of light from source to detector, and it generates an output that paper is OK; but in case of break, the light enters the detector, and it generates an opposite signal.

Within no time, the management started getting timely information about the runnability of the machine. Operators were being asked for each and every joint, probable reason and possible solutions. Yet, one operator who was more interested in doing the things as usual, found a solution to the 'problem'. Whenever he was in night shift, he fixed a piece of paper on to the sensor. Now the sensor cannot detect the web break, and the operator escaped from any questions.

The solution needed to be found out. It was observed that there was a blower that needed to be switched off when there is a paper break. So, a signal from that blower motor switchgear was taken and an electrical incandescent bulb was mounted outside the production hall in such a way that the bulb got illuminated when there was a paper break. Senior management, sitting from the office was able to know if paper machine is running smooth or not.

The objective of sharing this is to indicate that there are several 'check points' in machines, which can be used to monitor process effectively. The 'check points' concept was used at several places and showed positive results. I must also share another similar case here.

One day, we noticed that the production in the night shift was lower than the target production. On enquiry from paper machine shift in-charge, he told, "Sir, there was problem from boiler house. Steam pressure reduced several times. Due to this paper produced had high moisture and the same had to be discarded and sent for re-pulping." Obviously, the boiler operator was called, who presented different version, "Sir, there was some problem from the machine itself. The boiler operation was perfectly alright. At boiler house, pressure always remained more than 8.5 bar(g).

A simple solution as on today could be installation of online steam pressure recorder. But for a small mill 20 years back was something not economically affordable.

As a low cost solution, a steam pressure switch was installed in the steam line from boiler to paper machine. The machine required a minimum of 4.0 bar(g) pressure, so the switch was set for 5.5 bar(g). The output of pressure switch was connected to two indicating lamps (one each at boiler and paper machine section) and one time totalizer (Hour meter). The total cost involvement in this setup was nearly Rs.2500-3000 or so. Now, in case pressure reduces below 5.5 bar(g), the reading of time totalizer will increase indicating that the responsibility of the production loss was from boiler house. Otherwise, it is the paper machine department who has to explain. The system was shown to both in-charges, and needless to say, false blaming from any side stopped permanently.

Blame game can be controlled easily if you could find out and implement various 'check points' between the departments.

# Profitability Evaluation on Real Time

You are running a business, and your aim is to make profits. There are a number of businesses who do good work, seem very profitable but collapse suddenly after some time. Many businesses depend on balance sheets to know their profits and operating margins etc.

While working for a small mill – a family owned unit-, I was also looking after the administration and procurements. The mill had set up just a few months back, and I noticed that the inventory levels were declining. After some more time, when I discussed to procure anything, the counter reply was, "Do consider if you can delay the decision. We are running short of funds. We must first pay the monthly installment of financial institution." All sources of getting loans had already been used.

The case was discussed with the general manager, who in those times, acted like CEO of the mill. He convinced all that he had checked the operations thoroughly and there should be an operating profit of at least 8-10%. In no case it can go below 5%. If you are facing some financial troubles, please check if you are getting payments from all your consumers, maybe there are a lot of consumers who are not paying in time. Needless to say, marketing and sales was looked after by us only.

In fact, I was not convinced with his reply. For a person with technical education background, with interest in machinery related issues, understanding economics is something boring. However, considering it a serious matter, I decided to do something. Next whole day, I spent making a model of the system. I identified several heads- Waste paper, chemicals, Electricity (diesel for DG sets), Boiler fuel, and worker salary, Interest of financial institution, consumables and stores.

While you have a little inventory, consumption measurement is not an issue. I took production figures and waste paper consumption figures for past month, and the ratio gave the yield. Similarly, per ton of paper chemical consumption, boiler fuel consumption etc. were obtained. As there was no electricity supply, the plant was being operated on electricity from DG sets. So, diesel cost was taken as electricity cost. All minor consumables and store items were decided to be taken as per actual.

In a plant, you need some costly consumables, like rolls, machine clothing etc. The cost of each of these divided by expected production per item gave an approximate idea about these costs. All such items were added up and a new word, "fixed" was considered.

Now, with this, the concept became simple to implement. Take production figure in the morning; calculate waste paper, chemical, boiler fuel costs etc., and simple arithmetic gave the profit. But the problem was that it was not profit. It was 'loss'- a loss to the tune of more than 15%. I checked the calculations again and again, but, nothing seemed incorrect. Finally, I decided to check again the next day. For three days, I did the same exercise, and the figures were almost the same. So, I asked one of the directors to cross check and guide me if there is some mistake. But the calculations were correct.

The matter was raised in the next board of directors meeting which was called immediately to discuss the issue. On the basis of these calculations, it was clear that the mill needed to act fast and take necessary steps to control the cost of production. The data were compared to industry benchmarks, and electricity consumption appeared as a major bottleneck. A reputed energy audit company was contacted, but they offered a short go through audit that too after 15-20 days. They suggested that after the report of short audit, detailed audit shall be planned and thus the whole process was going to take nearly 3-4 months. The mill cannot afford to wait so long, so it decided to contact some consultants and in-house evaluation to reduce energy consumption. Within 3 months, the specific electricity consumption could be brought down to one third.

Meanwhile, efforts were initiated increase production. By this, fixed costs were expected to decrease. All these efforts clubbed together were able to bring mill from 15% operating losses to nearly 5-7% operating profits that too within 4-6 months.

Now the policy is to evaluate profit/loss statement on a daily basis. This helps a lot in making timely decisions to ensure maximum profitability, and taking steps to further improve upon the same.

# Inter-Department Tussle

This happened when I was working for a large scale company. Good management practices demand that the production losses must be monitored department wise. This creates a healthy competition between different departments to reduce downtime and thus increase production. Obviously, if you are going to change some machine clothing or some roll, and during that planned shut, some electrical or maintenance work is done, then the whole mill gains. But in this case something opposite took place.

In the mill, there were different departments, and the whole team was very attentive towards reducing the downtime. It happened during night shift, where there was some electrical problem in one of VFD. Mr. Sunil Sharma was there in the mechanical department. Sunil was considered one of the most brilliant electrical engineer in his level. When I went there, Sunil was sitting on the floor in front of a VFD opened up fully. I asked, "How much time you think it would take?" He replied, "Don't know. It is difficult to say anything at this stage."

Sometime later, I asked the machine foreman to check what he is doing. The foreman informed, "Sir, he has opened three drives, many electrical parts are spread on the floor, and he has said to his assistant, that it may be morning before he is able to fix the problem.

Quite obviously, I decided to take the benefit of the situation. We needed to change the paper machine felt, which needs nearly 3 hours of down time. So, the old felt was cut immediately, and the procedure to mount the new felt was initiated. Within 30-35 minutes, Sunil's assistant appeared and informed that the electrical problem had been solved and you may run the machine. Now the whole downtime after his intimation had to be reported for process department- for my department.

Next morning, I reported the case to my senior, Mr. Goel. Mr. Goel had prior information about this as well as others such incidences by Sunil earlier also. He suggested me to be careful in future in case Sunil is in the same shift as of mine. He further suggested that in case such situation appears again, "Just don't do anything. If shut takes too long, mention in log book that you were not indicated that this electrical fault may take so long to solve."

To me, Sunil was not the real problem. I think the real problem is to find the way to deal with such activities so that the healthy atmosphere is not lost.

# Compressor Operation

While starting a paper mill in 1998, two compressors were installed. The compressors were of K G Khosla make, which is still considered to be the best compressor supplier existing that time. Each compressor was having a capacity of 35 cfm, and produced air at 9 bar(g) pressure. These compressors were reciprocating type. To control the air pressure, these were fitted with a pressure switch so in case the pressure reached 9 bar(g), the compressor stopped and if the pressure reduced to 8.5 bar, it started again.

In around year 2000, when we decided to take energy conservation at top priority, to monitor the performance, time totalizer (hour meter) were installed on both the compressors. Now, daily reading difference could indicate how much each compressor operated in a day. Typical figures were 18 hours. That meant we needed nearly 50-52 cfm air for our plant, as calculated from capacity multiplied by run hours multiplied by number of compressor divided by 24 hours.

While taking energy conservation efforts in the utility section, we began with leakage arresting. Liquid soap solution was prepared in a bucket, and with the help of sponge, it was applied on each and every joint in pipeline. Any bubble formation was indicating that there was some leakage of air. In the next shut, these leakages were arrested. Most of the leakages seemed so minor that the maintenance fitters were not initially interested to attend these. They said, "Sir, this is just very small. How much air can be released from this rate? Let's leave it as it is." But, we marked each leakage hoping to reduce to run hours below 10 hours a day for each compressor.

After the machine started, we waited anxiously to see the results of compressor run hours. Next day, when the shift electrician reported (yes, it was electrician duty to report all hour meter readings), we could not believe at glance. The run hours were 2.3 and 2.8 for both compressors. That meant, more than 85% of air was earlier being leaked to atmosphere and only less than 15% was being used for the machine.

With time, we observed some bonuses. As the compressors were running less, the maintenance –oil change, valve replacement etc. reduced significantly. There was no air dryer though most air used was for instruments purpose, yet due to reduced air moisture, -as the compressed air has a longer retention time in reservoir- the life of FRL, clutches, regulators and even pneumatic cylinders increased significantly.

Leaks! Though might look small, but pose a significant loss to your profits.

# Balance Production

What happens if you produce, but do not report in time? You cannot take the difference of production to your home. But in case there is some down time, you may choose not to disclose it. The management does not know what is really going on in the plant. This way, management becomes incapable of taking decisions to maintain its existence and the mill closes.

In a paper mill, the production people asked electrical people to adjust display of 'speed meter' to a lower value. While the paper machine was being operated at 250 mpm (meter per minute), the display showed 240 mpm. This way, nearly the mill was producing nearly 4% more production that was generally being reported.

The process men were right in their opinion. "We are not taking any production at our home. Whatever we have produced will remain here." It was appearing also. For example, at the end of any shift, the production was say 11 MT. But surplus cumulative production was 5.0 MT. Now, there was some problem in the paper machine dryer section. That resulted in 1.5 hour production loss. Instead of reporting the same, they indicated the same 11.0 MT production in log book, and informed that the balance production was 3.5 MT. Every shift, they were getting almost 0.4 MT balance increase, and for any downtime they could be asked to explain they reduced the balance production to shrug off their responsibility.

Slowly and slowly the balance production became so important in their life that the machine head was more interested in knowing this rather than the production itself at the end of shift.

While the management cannot get proper information about the plant performance, it cannot take right decisions. While I took over as unit head in a small mill started after this incident, my main aim was to ensure that mill reporting is accurate. Reporting formats were redesigned in such a way that the parameters monitored were correct. Still, many of the staff members considered it as a breach to their freedom.

The major benefit appeared when I decided to monitor joints in paper production. Well, if you are producing paper to the tune of 25 ton per day, and there is a joint in paper, and you re-reel the paper, nearly 5 minutes of production is lost. That is nearly 100 kg of paper lost. According to that time economics, you may say that 100 kg of paper has become as waste paper in just one joint. That costs typically Rs.1000, as computed that time. So, we started saying that "One joint costs Rs. 1000 to the mill". This created some awareness in production people.

The next step was to monitor all joints. A group of dedicated persons was deputed to check all joints, with the duration and possible reason for the whole month. They started noting down every joint. Often the papermakers changed the roll so that the joint is not recorded. But, checkers kept on noting down each and every joint. After the paper resumed after the joint, the checkers asked what the reason of this joint was, and noted their observations also.

Within a month the picture was clear. There were more than 900 joints, with more than 80% of the joints due to a single reason (slime). So far the papermaker used to say, "Sir, in steel plants, steel sheets do break, this is just paper", but after this detailed study, he was also convinced that if we are able to solve the problem of slime we can reduce the number of joints to one fourth.

The observations were discussed with some industry experts, specialty chemical suppliers, and after the solution was found out, the number of joints decreased to around 250 per month.

After some time, I asked him, "Do you think we could have reached to less than 250 joints per month from 900+ joints per month, if you were keeping on reporting the managed data?" I think I need not tell his answer.

If you need to control anything, you need to monitor it properly. Consider that as a prerequisite.

# Magnetic Fuel Saver

Long back, when the electricity generation prices from diesel (HSD) were less, and state grid electricity prices were higher, we used to run the plant with DG sets only. We initiated monitoring the DG sets performance very closely. We observed that for a load range of 40% to 90%, the specific electricity generation was 3.68 kWH per liter of diesel. This gave a fair idea about the performance of DG sets. In fact daily average varied slightly in the range of 3.6-3.8 kWH/lit. Regular monitoring of the same was very useful, as in case of slightest reduction in fuel economy, we were able to take decision like air filter needs cleaning/replacement, or some other parameter needs to be monitored.

Later some supplier came to us suggesting procuring a magnetic fuel saver for us. This was nothing but a strong permanent magnet of specific shape, which is supplied in two pieces, and clamped to cover over the pipeline to DG set. He informed that the strong magnetic field of more than 25000 gauss will separate the ions of diesel, due to which atomization of diesel in the combustion chamber will increase. The overall result will be nearly 3-5% less fuel consumption. For a 380 kVA set, running at almost full (90% load continuously), this could mean a saving of around 2500 liters of diesel every month. The price of unit was around Rs. 25,000 so the payback was in less than a month considering a price of Rs.10-15 per liter of diesel those days.

Many mills had reportedly installed this saver, and some had even issued the supplier a letter that they were very satisfied with this equipment. However, I insisted upon producing a detailed report of some installation, which he produced after a few days. That installation was done in an engineering goods manufacturing company.

On thorough investigation of the report, it was clear that the mill had installed the system on a day; and on the same day some process modifications were also made. As a result, there was 3% reduction in their electrical load. The operating load in amperage showed this, the shift wise kilowatt load also indicated this. Cleverly, the consumption per shift was indicated for 15 days prior to and 15 days after the installation. When checked thoroughly, it was clear that the kWH per ton of diesel remained the same. Obviously, the fuel consumption was also reduced to the same extent, 3%. This indicated that the reduction of fuel was not due to the saver, but due to reduction in electricity consumption.

I further asked few questions-, "If the system is so useful, why don't the DG manufacturer mandatorily install it in new DG sets, and start claiming lesser diesel consumption? Obviously, this could give them an edge over their competitors." And, interestingly, "HSD (Diesel) is a non-ionic substance. How the ions of the same can be separated mere in the presence of magnetic field?"

Anyway, later found, the idea was very successful for the sellers, and they were able to gain millions of rupees by selling the toy, -a small piece of magnet- to many customers.

# Empty Soap Box Problem

Most of you must have heard of empty soap box problem. One soap manufacturing got a complaint that in one carton, the customer found a soap box which was empty. Considering company's name and fame, the issue was taken seriously, and the provision was made that each soap box moved on a conveyor belt, and using online X-ray scanners, the contents were started being checked. To check thoroughly, a monitor was installed and a quality control person was deputed over there.

The similar case happened with another company. They made the same arrangement, but instead of installing X-ray scanner, they mounted one exhaust fan near the conveyor. Thus, the soap box filled with soap remained in place, while the empty soap box was thrown away by the force of air.

We have heard this story in many whatsapp messages. In case, we are running a soap manufacturing factory, and face a similar situation, we all know what we'll be doing. But, if something similar or dissimilar is the case?

A similar situation I observed in a paper mill. The chemical dosing was being done in paper to maintain some specific property. The dosing pump was reciprocating type. Due to some problem, the hose pipe carrying chemical from one end to other got jammed, and the chemical could not reach to the pulp. During hourly testing, the problem was noticed, but by then one hours production was made off-quality and hence rejected.

During the day, we discussed a lot about installation of flow switch, magnetic flow meter or something, but discussions could not end, and the issue was postponed for a day. Next day, on reaching the mills, I observed a piece of paper (normal A4 size) hanging with a big circle and 'X' mark on it. The paper seemed tied with strings at both ends, and it was fluttering. On reaching near to it, everything was clear. The one end was tied to the hose pipe carrying the chemical. Due to reciprocating action of the pump, there were vibrations, and these were easily visible as the paper was fluttering. If the pump stops, or due to any other problem the chemical movement stops, the paper fluttering will stop and the operator will know about it.

Looking at that 'X' mark on the paper often reminds me that we were unable to learn anything from the 'Empty Soap Box Problem' story. Our operator learnt, and implemented the correct solution well within time.

# Boiler Energy Audit

Long back we were facing problems with the boiler that the fuel consumption is high. In case of a high fuel consumption, there could be many possibilities- plant steam consumption is high, boiler is not operating at desired air flow, thus resulting in inadequate combustion, there is scaling in boiler etc. Having no idea about it, we decided to go in for boiler audit, and sent enquiries to several auditors.

It took nearly 15 days to receive offers from different firms and finalizing the order. After the order finalized, the auditor informed that his team will visit after another 20 days with all necessary instruments. The team made several measurements, fuel and ash analysis, collected samples of the same for further evaluation in their laboratory, tested feed water, make up water and blow down water for the properties etc. This continued for a couple of days and afterwards they went back. We waited more than a one month to get the boiler energy audit report from them.

The report was detailed, with a lot of data, a lot of calculations and a lot of suggestions. They suggested short term and long term measures. In a way, it was in ideal energy audit report. I myself am "Certified Energy Auditor", and the report was meeting all my expectations fully.

However, looking from a CEO point of view, I was not satisfied at all. Everyone knows the boiler fuel must be dry. High moisture means increased fuel consumption. But, if I am not getting dry fuel particularly in rainy season, I am helpless. Everyone knows there should be theoretically no excess air in boiler, as the extra air supplied takes heat off the boiler that go along with the boiler exhaust through the stack. On the other hand, inadequate air will result in incomplete combustion and hence more fuel consumption. Finally, what does the boiler efficiency mean? The boiler efficiency is just an indicative figure of overall efficiency of boiler as a team of company's management, capability of boiler equipment, capability of boiler operator, type of fuel being used, percentage condensate return etc.

What do I need? If I am operating a particular boiler, a particular fuel with a particular moisture content etc., let us keep these variables as fixed. Now, what an operator can do? He can adjust dampers of ID fan and FD fan to achieve most efficient operation. One operator runs boiler say at 25% excess air, while the others at 10% and 50% excess air respectively. If at 10% excess air, the combustion is not adequate (maybe due to some problem with boiler air handling system design), and we get best results at 25%, to the management the first operator is most efficient. Secondly, if we are able to get this information for different type of fuels, we may identify the most efficient operator for the boiler.

Similarly, if for a particular fuel and best operator (to maintain optimum air-fuel ratio), I am able to get 'X' efficiency while the other boiler can achieve 'X+Y' efficiency, I can easily say that replacing my existing boiler will give me the advantage of 'Y' efficiency. So, we need to break efficiency into three sectors-

1. Boiler management efficiency
2. Boiler operator efficiency
3. Boiler equipment efficiency

I must, further, add that fuel is often chosen as per the availability and other factors concerned. In rainy season, if you are getting bagasse or rice husk with a very high moisture content, you have no other option. The operator efficiency plays a major role. Similarly, the boiler as equipment needs to be evaluated for its efficiency so that timely actions for its modification or replacement may be taken.

# First Fire Accident

Long back, on a day, I noticed small fire at one state owned electrical sub-station installed near to the mills. Those times, the mobiles were not so common and I had one. I made a call to district fire office, as there was no fire station in that city. They asked everything- my name, my phone number from where I was calling. I had to tell the mobile number twice. Meanwhile, we decided to shut the plant and depute all the workers for fire safety. The fire could be extinguish within half an hour or so.

After nearly one and a half hour, the fire tender appeared. By this time, the workers had went back to their jobs and plant had resumed production. The fire officers went to the mills office. After a few minutes, one of the directors came searching for me, and asked if I had informed them of fire. I accepted. On this he asked me to immediately switch off my mobile, took the same from me, and asked me to hide somewhere in the plant- rather behind the boiler house. He further told me not to come out and he will send my lunch there itself. Confused, I agreed.

After an hour or so, he came back to me, and informed that the fire officers wanted a sum of Rs. 35,000 from him. The expenditure from district headquarter to the site for one trip of fire tender costs that much, according to the fire officers. They were saying that the intimation was made from that company, by some of the employee of that company so he will have to pay. He tried to convince them that the phone call was indeed made to help a government department (electricity sub-station) in the national interest, and the person who called you actually did a good job, but in vein. Finally, after a lot of negotiations, the director had to pay Rs. 12,000 to them. Anyway, the director did not say that my decision of informing the fire office was wrong, or in future I should not inform them in case of similar fire incident.

On hearing about this, I felt sorry, In fact, in place of sorry, I should use the word, 'bad' here. Anyway, the matter ended and I started forgetting this. More than 12-14 years passed but whenever I felt necessary I informed the fire department. But last year I heard about a fire accident case through the newspapers. Fire broke up in a hospital in Kolkata. The fire was so severe that more than 60-70 people including many kids (several newborn) died in it. Unfortunately, no one from the hospital informed the fire station timely about the incident. Those days, this was a big issue, and suddenly a small piece of news caught my attention. The news indicated that around a week earlier, a smaller fire broke in the same hospital, which was being intimated by one of the security guards to fire office. He raised alarm, and fire was attended by the staff of the hospital. Finally, when the fire tender arrived, the staff had already put off the fire. The next day, that security guard was removed from duty by the management.

While everyone was blaming that hospital of Kolkata and its management for the irresponsible behavior and approach in fire management, in a small corner of my heart, there was something pinching. Did something similar to what happened to me happen there? Had the hospital management actually forced to pay some money or bribe; or some lives? Otherwise, what was the reason that the management took a very harsh decision just because a security guard intimated the fire office? I recalled a simple statement read somewhere about the fire, "World's largest fires could have been extinguished with just a cup of water, if it was poured at the right place and right time."

I wish anybody who reads this, should always be sympathetic to our lower grade workers, who really love their workplace and may inform the concerned officers in the very beginning of any fire accident. Taking action in such situations must always be followed after considering about the probable consequences.

# Capacitor Installation on DG sets

The mill had three DG sets, each one of 380 kVA. Two were required at a time and the third one was standby. Slowly and slowly, as the efforts were going on to increase production, to improve quality, the load was increasing. Now, there were two possibilities- either run the third DG set also or explore the possibilities to increase the load on running DG sets to maximum.

Fitted with a six cylinder of 1150 ml, turbocharged, after-cooled, these Cummins KTA-1150-G DG sets were considered best DG sets in their class. The alternator was Stemford make with an SX-400 AVR installed. On detailed discussions with experts, we observed that the engine was designed for operating at full load without any problem with up to 10% overload for one hour in 24 hours. On the other hand, the alternator was suitable for 504 ampere current. We further observed that the same engine was being used for radiator cooled sets as well as heat exchanger mounted sets. That means, the design calculations included the load of radiator fan also, which must be 8-10kW or more.

For the same, we decided to operate the DG sets on increased load. We knew that the rated load was 304kW, but as we are using heat exchangers, by avoiding the radiator fan, we could go up to 310-315kW safely. But the problem appeared with the current. Now, as the radiators are designed for 0.8 power factor, we decided to install capacitors, to increase power factor to 0.95. The basic aim was to reduce the current load so that the $I^2R$ losses in alternator as well as in distribution lines were expected to decrease.

The approach worked well. Next month, the average operating load was 306 kW. The set was operated for 717 hours in a month of 30 days- more than 99.5% uptime, except for routine servicing etc.

Hearing about our results, a nearby mill also installed capacitors. But next time, when the service engineer visited, he flatly asked them to remove capacitors, otherwise the company might cancel the warranty of DG set. The service engineer had his own version. He said that the current being displayed on DG panel becomes false when you install capacitor. Capacitor cannot generate current (ampere), it just absorbs the current and hence DG sets had to bear more loads. On referring my name, he came to our plant and started asking DG operators and electricians where have they installed the capacitors. They refused that saying that we have not installed any capacitor on DG set. (The installation was done in the electrical PCCs).

For the safety, the issue was discussed with senior experts of DG supplier. After long discussions, they agreed with our point.

If you want to do anything abnormal, it is always better to discuss the issue with supplier experts. Most of the time, the service engineer is not the right person for this.

# Fan Pump Pulley

Fan pump is the pump with maximum flow rate in most of the paper mills. The head of the pump was usually lower as the machine speeds were low. This way, the pump works as a fan- high throughput and low head. Probably this was the reason that the fan pump got its name.

In most of the projects, the pumps are overdesigned considering too high a factor of safety. The end result is the increased power consumption when the plant comes in operation. Considering this, it was decided to install a VFD to reduce power consumption. The earlier motor was of 55 kW running at 98 ampere load (full load). A telephone call was made to a supplier who indicated that the VFD shall cost Rs. 4 lakhs or so.

As the mill was in financial crisis, the investment proposal was immediately rejected. However, another effort was made and the supplier was asked if we are sure that the load will reduce, can we install a VFD for 40 kW on this pump? If yes, what would be the price? The price now was 2 lakhs. But, this proposal, despite being indicated that the payback would be just a couple of months or so, was rejected. To many, this may seem illogical now, but, there are several situations when you do not have finances, and the possibility of taking loan and advances from all sources have been consumed fully. Anyway, this was the time to think for something else- something within the resources.

A step was taken. We decided to lift the motor up and a frame was prepared using scrap material. Now instead of direct tyre coupling, v-pulleys of calculated size were mounted on both pump and motor. V-belts were mounted, and the speed of fan pump was reduced. The total investment for pulleys and v-belts was Rs. 4500 or so. The whole process took nearly 3 hours, and the same was done during a routine plant maintenance shut, thus no additional downtime was made.

When the machine started, the load on the pump had reduced from 98 amperes to 52 amperes (29 kW). That meant nearly 25 kW saving. Typical payback was 2-3 days only. After a few years, we installed a VFD, and could save another 4-5 kW.

Now, when I look back, I often feel that making heavy investments is generally preferred and we ignore the possibilities of using the basic fundamentals. If you have to operate the pump at a fixed speed (or vary the speed within a narrow range); you should also consider such low cost options.

# Start of PaperTechnology Group

Long back, we noticed that there were several problems in the plant, appearing one by one. Initially some consultants were hired and they made one or two visits every month, and the issues were discussed with them. To a certain extent, this helped, but later we started feeling the burden of the same. Meanwhile, we decided to install a new high consistency pulper. To begin with, we wrote letters to several suppliers to send their offer for the same. The letters were simple, hand written, indicating the approximate capacity of the same.

Next day, the consultant visited the mill. The matter was discussed and seeing the carbon copy of the letter, he said that the enquiry should be written giving full details. He further indicated that he himself will draft a letter in our name, and send enquiry to one most reputed supplier.

Next week I got an offer from the supplier in return to my enquiry. A few days letter, I got another offer from the same supplier in return to the consultant's enquiry. But the both the offers were different. Both offers suggested the same design and model of the pulper, but the second offer excluded a few items, and was priced nearly 10% higher. Comparing both offers on even grounds, there was more than 17-18% price difference. It could be anything-consultant's commission or overcharging from smart potential buyer who has drafted a beautiful letter.

Slowly and slowly, we started feeling that we need some external help in running the plant more and more efficiently. A few other friendly mills came up with an idea that a group of even minded mills should be made, and the manager of one mill will visit the other mills periodically. Seems a good idea, but there were possibilities of head hunting that could not be ruled out this way.

Other constraints were movement of the person from mill to mill, different qualities being made by different mills etc. If I am making a very good quality paper and the other is not, my manager can give inputs and knowledge to the other, but that would not happen vice versa. We needed a solution that was something better, something safer, something useful something practical.

A few days later the idea of Yahoo groups appeared. This seemed interesting, so I formed a group named "PaperTechnology" with just five or six likeminded people. Initially, we discussed a couple of small points related to our mutual interest, and after finding it useful, we began starting others. Within a couple of years, the membership rose to 100. By this time, the group started gaining popularity and in next couple of years, we rose to 365.

The group was being very useful to the members. Members posted their day to day problems, like the production loss due to insects and flies coming in machine hall during rainy season, and got practical solutions from other members who had witnessed the similar problems. Earlier, no platform was able to provide such information.

But now, the group was active for past five years, but another problem started appearing. Group functions were getting disturbed. Earlier, if some spam or unwanted message got posted, I deleted that, and everything was normal. But, some messages started appearing again even after deletion. Several members complained that their posts were not going online. This continued for two or three months. Meanwhile another problem started appearing. The members with other email ids were unable to connect to Yahoo groups. Probably Yahoo wanted that only the people with Yahoo id should get access to Yahoo groups. So, even against the wish of some members, I decided to move to Facebook.

I wrote personal email to all members indicating the problems with Yahoo group server, message posting problems etc. and send them the link to facebook group. On facebook, the response was superb. Within a year, the membership rose to 1000. Next year it rose to 1800-1900. My administration rules were clear-

Only posts related to Pulp & Paper Technology are allowed.
No greetings at all. No Happy Birthday, Happy New Year etc.
No advertising on the group.

I recall removing several members just for continuing posting of irrelevant messages.

Later, as a step to move it forward, the group was handed over to IPPTA (Indian Pulp & Paper Technical Association).

The group itself gave a lot of knowledge. People, rather professionals do help each other. When we faced any issue related to quality of paper, and posted the problem; within 24 hours, we received many replies. A couple of member, who were shy to post anything, made a phone call to tell what should be done to solve that particular problem.

Make the best use of networking. Most professionals like to support others in their problems.

# DG Alternator failure

The mill was running on DG sets of 380kVA each. There were five DG sets, out of which normally three were used at a time. One a day, alternator of DG flashed off. This was a big issue, but not making much effort to identify the possible reason behind this, we just sent it to a winding person, and mounted another one kept as spare on the same DG set.

After three or four days, it flashed again. Now, this was serious. Well, we decided to remove alternator from DG no. 5 as cabling from that could be difficult, and mount it on DG no. 3. Instructions were given to all operators to ensure that the load does not increase beyond 450 amperes, against the rated load of 504 amperes. After the set started, we began to discuss the matter with many people.

We had sent one alternator to a local winder, while the second was sent to a reputed winding firm which was authorized by the supplier. We decided to go to the second firm next day while he had dismantled the alternator. I asked about the possible reason of the failure of the same. We got mixed reactions. One winder said there was a possibility that the insulation got weak. His partner said it could be due to sudden high current or jerk load. One thing we were all sure. It had been operated below 80% of rated load. We further asked how we can check the strength of insulation periodically so that such failures can be avoided in future and we may plan a preventive action in time. But, reportedly, such methods were also not available.

Two alternator failures and we had no clue at all. Discussions with electrical engineers, consultants, motor and alternator winding experts resulted in no conclusion. Meanwhile, third alternator flashed. Now this was enough to blow fuses of our mind.

Something had to be done, and that must have been done fast, but what?

I decided to investigate alone. After 6:00 PM, when everyone left- all directors, HODs, unit electrical head etc., I asked one person to call all shift DG operators. One was on duty, while the other two were called. The alternator failures occurred one in each one shift. Then I asked security team to ensure they sit in separate rooms and do not talk with each other. I called one of them and asked if he noticed anything suspicious or abnormal on the day of failure? Initially, he looked a little frightened. But I assured him that I am not blaming anyone, but want to find out the basic reason of the failure. He could not recall any. Then I explained him that this was a serious issue. "Imagine if we are unable to solve the problem, the whole factory becomes non-operative. More than 100 workers, their families would suffer. We jointly have to think, and identify the problem. A small clue, a small hint from you could indicate towards the source of the problem." He appeared thinking, but was unable to recall. So, I sent him to another room to think more, and called the second one.

The same discussions took place with the second one, but in vein. Then exactly the same thing happened with the third. I asked a peon to arrange for dinner/tea to them if they need, as it was around 8:30. Meanwhile I went to DG hall. I observed some littering on the DG cooling water pipeline. Pigeons used to sit on these lines, and hence these were dirty. I too could not find any reason for the problem.

Then the second round started. I asked about the pigeon litter and questioned if failures took place when there were more pigeons? Obviously, they smiled and said no. Then I told them to not worry about stupidity of thinking. I had quoted the example for you to recall every minute change or observation so that we may get some clue. However, second round failed again.

Then the third and probably the last round started. I knew if I could not get a clue, I had to explore some other ways to find out the reasons, but I did not know "what". I too had started feeling tired, and a little hopeless, but the operator immediately on entering the office said, that he recalled that he noticed sometimes the frequency dropped to less than 43-44 Hz. This was a big clue for me. I further enquired, why this was not being reported in your log books, and his answer was "the problem of low frequency appeared just for a few -5 or 7 seconds- that too in odd times like 6:45 pm or so. But they report the ampere, voltage, frequency etc. at 6:00AM, 7:00AM, 8:00AM… or so." Well the problem was the printed format. I asked why he did not mention it in "Remarks:" section, but he said that he did not consider that as important point that time and thought it was just usual.

The other operators, when asked, confirmed the issue, quoting the same reason. Now I had a big clue. It was 11:00 at night, and there was dense fog in some midway of December. I decided to ensure if this could be a cause of alternator flashing. So, I took a bike (cars are difficult to move through narrow lanes in old city) and went to our winders home and called him.

He woke up and came outside. I explained him the whole situation and asked, "Can DG frequency reduction be a reason for alternator failure?" He said yes, and then explained "Due to low frequency the field current increases and hence it may result in exciter flashing leading to finally alternator failure." To solve the problem of low frequency, he suggested getting the engine fuel pump checked at the service center. I thanked him, and left for my home.

Next day, we sent the fuel pump to the authorized service center. In the evening, they called me. That fuel pump had been generating very little pressure due to extreme wear. The service engineer told me that against the minimum permissible pressure of 9.5 bar, we normally used to get 10-10.5 bar when the pump is sent for servicing. But this time, the pressure was just 6.5 bar. On asking for the reason, he indicated that the fuel quality might be poor.

Oh yes! We had started buying HSD (diesel) from some other supplier for the past few months. On discussion with engine experts, they told that the fuel supplied by that company lacked lubrication and hence the fuel pump performance deteriorated soon. This diesel was nearly 8-10% cheaper compared to earlier suppliers.

The problem which we were considering as electrical one was being caused by a mechanical reason originally generated from procurement decision.

# DG Abnormal Sound

While we started the plant, we had no good DG operators. Many a times, when you start a new mill, manpower shortage is often a problem. The DG supplier suggested a good formula. He told us how to start and stop the DG, and in case of any abnormal sound or any other problem, just call the service engineer. Under warranty period, his services were free, while after the warranty period, we could pay for the visits. We agreed. Slowly and slowly, our DG operators (all of them were new, untrained operators) became familiar with the DG sets. Within six months, they learnt from the service engineer how to replace fuel and lube oil filters, do the routine servicing jobs etc. Things started getting smoother.

Years passed, and we got a lot of advantage due to our lack of knowledge. In case of any slightest problem, we did not hesitate to call the service engineer. We were using only the genuine parts, and hence the breakdowns were negligible. Those newcomers who came to us searching for jobs few years ago were now the best DG operators in the district, as informed by the service engineers.

Suddenly, in the morning, a service engineer heard some abnormal sound, and he immediately shut the engine down. Afterwards, he called me and informed the incidence over phone. Those days, we had no mobile phones. As the service engineer was stationed at district headquartered, I sent a car to pick him up, and informed him telephonically about the problem and to be ready to leave as the car reaches.

Within 2 hours, he reached the mill, and asked the DG operator to start the set. The operator had gone to have a cup of tea, and the assistant operator started the engine. Meanwhile the operator reached and shut the engineer saying "It has some abnormal sound". The service engineer said that he had came to investigate the problem and asked him to start the set again. The set was started again and the service engineer did not find anything abnormal with the sound. He asked to keep the set running and run it on load. But, again the same thing happened. Within two minutes, this operator switched off the DG set quoting abnormal sound.

That service engineer was a senior one and also was a little arrogant. He became annoyed with his behavior. By this time I had also reached factory. He came to my office and started shouting, how my operator was insulting him, a senior service engineer from the supplier company. I consoled him and requested him to open the engine tapet cover (covers mounted on the head of engine), just pretend to loose and tight some valves, push rods in front of the operator so that the operator feels confident. I assured him that so far this DG operator has been very attentive to DG sets, so even if you feel DG set is perfectly OK, just pretend that you checked the set thoroughly and there was no problem at all. Initially, he refused saying that it was not needed. The engine was perfectly ok. However, I requested the same, again asking this as a personal favor towards me from him.

Finally, he agreed, and opened all the six tapet covers. Inside head no. 3, one push rod was found bent. Now, the service engineer was surprised. This was a serious problem. This push rod was not available in district headquarter also, so it was decided to arrange it from another service center around 200 km away. Meanwhile, the issue was informed to our service center from where this case was spread to head office of the DG supplier company.

By the evening the DG set was operational and the plant started. The service engineer appreciated the good observation and strong decisions made by the DG operator. A couple of day letter, I got a phone call from Pune, where the DG supplier is located. The service head informed that they were getting problems where the DG sets were getting failed suddenly due to engine caesurae, and the cause was unknown. Timely decision by our operator in this case not only saved us from a major engine breakdown but also helped the DG supplier to know how the problem initiated. Needless to say, they made some changes in push rod and its loading system design, and such problems were solved completely.

# Pollution Abatement vs. Charity

What is a better form of worship- pollution abatement or charity or religion? I visited a mill in middle India long back. The mill was facing some issues related to energy conservation, quality and production, and they wished me to be there for a couple of days. When I reached, initially, we visited the plant, and I explained the possibilities that could be explored to save energy etc. In the evening we planned a visit to a temple there. The temple is very famous, and the mill owner donated Rs.1000 note in the donation box. I also made some donation, but I knew from this that he was a very pious person.

Next day, I asked them to show me the effluent treatment plant. The mill was large spread over large area, so ETP was located a little away from the plant. On reaching there, I found that the effluent treatment plant was shut. The owner proudly (yes, 'proudly') informed me that they keep the plant shut always and only when some pollution control department officer comes, the plant is immediately started. Personally, I do not like this type of approach. But, he was the owner, and it was his decision how to run the plant.

For next few minutes, I could not say a word. Suddenly the idea of attaching the ETP to his pious nature flashed in my mind. I asked him a question, "How much, annually, as a family, do you spend on charity?" He seemed puzzled with this irrelevant question. Before he could decide how to answer or even ask why I had asked such a question, giving a short pause, I asked another question, "How much, do you think you'd have to spend if you wish to run this ETP properly?"

Well, he was smart enough to understand my intention. Maybe he evaluated in his mind, and replied, "Deveshji, you are right. We had never thought about it earlier. You have raised a very valid question. Now, we'll run the ETP regularly." He immediately called his factory manager and ordered him to run the ETP regularly and continuously.

More than 8-10 years have passed to this incident. Still today whenever we talk, he often says that his ETP is now running because I motivated him that day.

For those who ignore pollution abatement, my question remains the same- "What is your annual charity budget, and what is your annual pollution abatement budget? Will the God be happier if you spend more on religion and pollute the environment for saving some money?

# Press Roll Bearing Failure

Any bearing failure costs the cost of the bearing, cost of the bearing sleeve and the cost of the production loss due to the same. The third part often may be much higher than the first two. In this case, the press roll bearing 22340K failed. On investigation, it was observed that the inner race cracked. As obvious, another bearing with a new sleeve was mounted, and the machine started.

After a month or so, it failed again. Slowly and slowly, bearing failure became a regular feature. The consumption increased to 1-2 bearing every month. The cost of bearing was Rs.25,000 or so. This was a huge bearing with 57kg weight. We considered procuring genuine bearing, but the cost was very high, and we felt unable to procure it.

I visited one of my friends in another paper mill, Mr. PK. I explained him the problem, and as usual, he suggested using genuine bearing of reputed make, saying that it was not very costly. According to him the genuine bearing might cost as little as Rs.95,000-97,000 or so. I flatly refused to even consider as we could not afford the same and insisted that he must give a solution feasible to my mill. He smiled, and asked me if sometimes, I observed that the bearing sleeve was mounted loose on the journal. I said yes. Long back once the sleeve was loosely fitted. Then he asked if the fitter who mounted the sleeve loose had to face any action? My answer was yes again. I informed that the general manager that time abused him a lot and even gave him a slap for the careless fitting of the sleeve.

He then told me that that slap is the reason of bearing failures. In fact, the earlier fitter did not fit the sleeve tight enough, so it moved on the roll journal, and the journal got damaged. But too strict an action against the fitter created a fear in the mind of fitters, and they started keeping the sleeve too tight. The over-tight sleeve resulted in stress on the inner race of the bearing, and as a result, it broke.

His justification seemed logical. He further gave several practical inputs on how to mount the bearings properly. We initiated those practices, and there were no breakdowns for six months. Again, then a bearing failed in the same way. So, it was the time to investigate. On inquiry, the mechanical head informed that he felt that the sleeves being fit this way were loose, so he, on a trial, got the sleeve of that bearing tightened. Now, he was fully convinced of the concepts suggested by Mr. PK. For the past more than a decade, there has not been a single bearing premature failure in that section.

Proper mounting of bearings plays a significant role in getting good life of bearings and reduced downtime costs.

# DG Spares Pricing

Most engineering equipment come with a detailed exploded diagram, with each section and each part name is marked separately. With many machines involving a lot of parts and sections, the number of items is large, and whenever you need some part of equipment, the normal procedure is to look at the exploded diagrams in the equipment manual for the part number, and check the list price of that particular part number in the price list.

The process becomes so tiring most of the times that you do not look beyond the routine process, and find out the list price and place an order for the same.

Once, I needed a coupling that couples diesel generator's engine to alternator. The coupling consisted of four parts- a piece that is mounted on engine, a piece that the mounted on alternator, a spacer ring and twelve pieces of rubber bush which help to maintain cushion between all these three parts.
The coupling was priced Rs. 27,000 or so. We know anything if you buy in pieces costs more. Just for curiosity, I decided to find out the cost of each part separately. Got the prices of first three parts, and then the cost of rubber bush was multiplied by 12 (there were twelve such bush in a coupling), made a sum of all the figures, and I could not believe- the figure was just around Rs. 18,000.

It was something against our believes. I checked again if there was some mistake at my end, but every figure was correct. So, I decided to place the order with all parts separately. Next day, I got the coupling, and that was mounted on the DG set.

Curious, I decided to explore the issue more. After 9000 hours of operation, DG sets need a complete checkup and all the head gaskets etc. need to be replaced. The complete set was priced Rs. 16,500 or so. Now, there were more than 20-22 different types of gaskets etc. On checking each item separately, the price was a little less than Rs. 7,500. So, I placed the order for the same also.

Next day, I got the phone call from the supplier's regional office, "Why did you made this PO so longer. You need a head gasket set, so place order in one line only." But, I refused to procure these items as a set. He told me that according to their system, these parts were not available in their stock, as these have never been procured, so, I'll have to wait for 8-10 days as the material had to be shipped from company headquarters to them. For this I agreed. Next day, there was a call from headquarters, enquiring why I placed the order that way. I explained them the whole situation saying that their price list has severe irregularities that need to be looked into. Anyway, we received the material after some time, and the scheduled servicing was done.

Later, as an initiative from the supplier company, it was decided that a two member high level team shall visit us for further discussions on this issue. To explain the matter in a better way, I started investigating the price list. Some critical parts involving more accuracy in engineering design and with costly metallurgy were much cheaper than those which required very little accuracy or the material cost was not much. During the meeting we discussed a lot of points, and they assured me that they shall revise the price list to make it more justifiable, but further requested me not to share my findings with other customers in the area.

More than 12 years have passed, but still while ordering spares, I strongly feel that one must cross check the possibility of getting spares in a set or individually. Still, I feel there are several mills where engineering or maintenance department raises indent to procure some item by item number and the procurement is done in a mechanical way. Such mills might be getting spares at better discount, but not surely at better price.

# Others vs. Automobile sector! Reliability issues

I often recall how we travelled 25-30 years ago, if we had to go somewhere 200-300 kilometers away. The routine was to send the car to service station a day prior to journey. On the travel day, the driver reached an hour earlier, checked the tyre pressure, lube oil level, water level thoroughly, before we started. Now the situations are changed. Whenever we want to go, we just go to the car, sit inside, ignition on and vroom.

Have you recalled those days' cars were not many? Still, it was not uncommon to see cars staying at the side of roads due to breakdown, like dynamo failure, engine overheating etc. Now, we have probably more than 10 times the cars, but breakdowns are seldom. The automobile industry deserves applause for such level of reliability achieved.

On the other hand, in most industries, such level of reliability is still a dream. With improved manufacturing facilities, better technologies, good automation, computer controlled (SCADA, PLC, DCS & QCS) systems we are much better than where we were earlier, still much has to be done.

For any bearing failure, the maintenance department may give several reasons. For every motor failure, the electrician may tell that the reason was overload or some other defect, for any pneumatic valve failure, you may have some reasons. But, every failure puts you away from maintaining reliability.

The basic objective of sharing this is to create awareness and focus to our efforts for creating such reliability in our respective fields.

# SuperCalender Cotton Roll

After coating, paper is passed between various rolls to make its surface smooth. This is done in supercalender. The rolls of the same are alternatively of chilled cast iron, and of cotton. The cotton rolls give the paper a soft backing while the polished chilled rolls give the smooth effect to paper surface. The whole action is like the ironing of the clothes.

When, in a new plant, the calender was first installed, the immediate problem was frequent burning of the roll surface. If a roll gets burnt, then you may grind it to remove its top surface, so that all the burnt material is removed; and reuse the roll for some more time. After several such grindings, normally the roll becomes useless and you need to send it back to supplier for refilling.

When the plant was started, initially, the mill had very less orders, hence production usually continued for a few days, followed by a shut for another few days for want of production orders. It became a routine practice that the rolls needed frequent grinding due to burning problem. Occasionally, the burning of the roll was so severe that the roll had to be discarded and sent again for coating. One day, while being too tired of frequent breakdowns, I called the supplier. He replied, "Sir, this is a new plant, you have installed the SuperCalneder for the first time. That is why you seem much worried. Please wait for some more time". I felt a little assured, but to confirm, asked again, "So, what will happen after some more time? Will the operators be more used experienced or we'll learn how to reduce such losses? If yes, do we need a training program on how to operate it better?" I thought that he will suggest that we should send our operators to send to their mills for some training, but he replied in other way, "No, after some time you will be habitual of this frequent burning problem of cotton rolls." It was

9:30 PM, and sat on a chair in front of roll grinding lathe, I found myself in the middle of nowhere.

That night, I could not sleep. We needed a solution to the problem of new equipment. By that talk it was clear that the supplier was not going to be helpful to me. Next day onwards, I started keeping a record of everything- everything that was or could be related to Super Calender. Within a month or so, I was able to detect something. Most roll burnouts occurred within first two hours of operation when the plant restarted after a shut of 2-3 days or more. Almost every time, the machine started, there was a roll failure. I called the production in-charge. I presented the data, and asked what could be the reason? He informed that the machine should be operated at low load without paper for first 1-2 hours so that the rolls are adapted to operating load and temperature. So, why were they not doing this? The reason was silly. They already knew it, but there was pressure from the dispatch people to calender the paper and load the truck after the paper was ready for calendering. That was obvious. When you get any order after a shut, people want to produce fast and dispatch the material at the earliest so that the consumer gets the material, consumes it fast, and release the further order.

This helped us reducing a big problem; however, a few rolls were also getting burnt now and then even after this. We decided to shift to a better supplier, but the results and performance could improve only slightly. The MD of second roll coating company himself visited and suggested us to maintain proper roll surface temperature. In case the temperature exceeds 80-85 deg Centigrade, we should run the supercalender at reduced speed and load. To certain extent, it seemed helping, but very little.

We tried searching information available on the internet, but detailed information related to this case was not available. So, I started studying about cotton. Cotton has a very special property. Under the atmosphere of high humidity, it absorbs moisture and in low humidity environment it loses some of its moisture content. This information gave a clue that the most roll failures should appear in low humidity season. This was a big clue. More than 2 years have passed, and we had plenty of records. All we needed to correlate the roll burning problem to temperature and humidity of atmosphere. The results were surprising. In humid summers (during rainy seasons of summer), there were very few failures, while the failures increased drastically during dry months of December and January. So far, we had correlated the issue with temperature alone, and probably this was the reason of prevailing failures.

It seemed if we could increase humidity during dry seasons, we shall definitely get some benefit. So, we planned some desert coolers. But the operators were not ready for the same. They had a fear that in case even a single drop of water goes along with the cool air from the cooler, the paper will break and thus causing production loss. All the four operators (three shift operators and a relieving operator) were described the situation, and convinced them about the benefits. We needed to do this because I had already observed that if you force a decision onto any operator, he may try to challenge you; but if he is brought into the loop of decision making, he always tries his best to get the best results.

The evaporative air coolers were installed and the same were very useful. The operating life increased from 800 hours per roll to 2000-2200 hours per roll. Still, we felt further improvement was possible. So, we considered addition of water in direct liquid form. A spray gun was procured and connected it with water and compressed air line. We decided to spray water on to the surface of the roll during periodic paper roll changes. The process was similar to spray painting your car. With this the roll life could be increased to over 3000 hours.

In case of working with some different material, having knowledge about the material and its properties is very helpful.

# Administration Vs. Research

During the initial phase of my professional career, I joined a reputed research institute as Senior Scientific Assistant. After a few days of my joining, one laboratory assistant demanded a paper cutting knife. Blotting pads were being used in lab for pressing small handsheets of paper made for testing purpose, and the blotting pads were tied with a plastic rope. The lab assistants wanted paper cutting knife for this purpose. Those days, the price of it could be just Rs.12 or 15 only. That seemed no issue to me, so I just filled and signed their 'store requisition slip' and sent to store. Unfortunately it was not available in store, so it was automatically indented by the stores department. I said to the lab assistants to wait for a couple of days for the procurement of it.

Next morning, the peon handed me over a long typewritten letter from FAO (Finance and Administrative Officer). It asked different questions related to the requirement-

- Give full detailed specifications of the instrument.
- The instrument you asked is required for which project- UNDP funded or Industry funded?
- Indicate the name of project for which it is required?
- If it is for an industry project, indicate whether the amount has to be charged to the mills or it shall be in our scope?
- Name some companies that manufacture this instrument. Give address, phone number, Telex Number and phone number of the manufacturer representative.

I was just reading the letter, and one senior scientist, who knew me well, entered in the lab. We had been very friendly, so I handed over the letter to him, asking what I should do now. He read it, smiled and asked, "Which razor do you use for shaving? Single blade? After two or three shaves, when the blade starts becoming blunt, just bring it here. These people can use that to cut the string. I do the same thing in my lab also."

I then asked him that I wanted a first aid box also in the lab. How should I proceed? He gave Rs. 100 from his wallet, saying that it was his contribution. I as well as other lab staff should contribute something and we can have a first aid box for us. After all it was needed for our own benefit. While I procured the first aid box and brought it with me to the lab, another similar situation was reeling in my mind.

Earlier, while doing engineering, one day, I went to computer lab. The monitor of a PC was dead. Maybe the fuse had blown. Anyway, I reported it in the complaint register and started working on other computer. Next day, the computer in-charge came to me and asked, why you wrote a complaint in the book. I told him that the monitor was dead, but why he was looking so tense over it. He said, "You know it well that the fuse has blown. The small glass fuse costs hardly 50 paisa or so. But, this is not there in our store. This university considers students complaints seriously. Now, as per rule, I'll have to write a letter to the HOD for procurement of the fuse. He will instruct me to go to the University headquarters (located in other city, around 60 km away) and get it from there. Against the requirement, I'll get one fuse, bring it back and make your computer monitor working. Don't worry, I'll get TA and DA for the same, but you can imagine how hard is it to spend the whole day out in this summer at more than 40 deg Centigrade. In addition, the University expenditure would be around Rs. 100 or so for just a fuse of 50 paisa" He further said, "If you had not mentioned it in the log book, I'd have purchased it from local market from my pocket and system was ok."

We spend a lot of money, time and efforts for maintaining 'systems' but often overlook to make these systems flexible and practical enough to avoid unnecessary troubles to those using these systems.

# Electricity Consumption, Wastage & Theft

During engineering, we did not face much electricity shortage issues. Though, it was not allowed, yet a few students were using heaters (to boil milk etc.) in their rooms. Many others had a habit of keeping the light and fan switched ON continuously even if they are not there in their rooms. I think, when you get something free of cost, it happens. I was also one of them then. My light and fan was also switched ON often, for which I feel sorry now.

Anyway, the hostel administration decided to install energy meters for the hostels. In our block, there were 12 rooms, six on ground floor, four on first floor and two on second floor. There were several blocks like this. As decided, two electricity meters –one for the ground floor and another one for first and second floor- were installed. Many of the students felt it bad. Within a couple of days, it was found that the meter indicated a power consumption of 12 kWH per day; so, on an average we computed 2 kWH per room per day. Someone made arrangements to remove the sight glass from this electromechanical meter cover and explained others how rotating the wheel in opposite direction can be used to reduce energy displayed. It was mutually agreed between the students of our block that each student will rotate the meter flywheel in reverse direction daily to reduce units by two.

Well, our group was too supporting for others. Each student thought of some other student, and did the work for other also in addition to doing his bit. Next month, I went to hostel supervisor office. He seemed a little annoyed with the work overload. He said, "These university people unnecessarily engage us in useless work. They asked to install electricity meters in each block. See, what we got- "Electricity consumption of minus 912 units in K-Block. University people cannot understand that these are engineering students."

After several years, I got a chance to visit a small unit, where the owners informed me that they were indirectly engaged in electricity theft. According to them, they did nothing wrong but when the meter reader came; he brought a remote with him and reduced the meter reading. The meter reader charged a couple of thousand rupees for a so called bill reduction for Rs. 5000 or so, every month. Now they want to me evaluate if the meter reader was reducing bill by 5000 or less. In fact, they had a doubt that the reduction in the meter was just Rs. 2000 to 3000, and the meter reader was 'overcharging' for meter adjustment.

I did a complete energy audit of the unit and found nothing wrong. The electronic temper-proof meter was sealed in such a way that any tempering was just impossible. I asked them to check the daily reading of the meter and to maintain a record for one month. Next month, I visited the same for evaluation of readings and the findings made us to smile. In fact, there was no theft at all. Meter reader usually came in the evening when everyone was in a hurry to leave for home. Before taking readings he used to take out his TV remote from bag, pressed a couple of buttons, noted down the readings, and collected his share. For past several years, the bribe was being given for electricity theft which was actually not being done.

When I club these cases together, I feel regular monitoring of any process is a must; otherwise it may lead to wastage. Monitoring system should be implemented in such a way that nobody can easily temper with it. And finally, the system should be such that all concerned may trust it.

I must confess one thing. During the fourth year of engineering, I had a habit of keeping the light and fan switched ON always. During attending classes, going to mess for meals, going to playground for sports, going to movies almost 2-4 times a week, every time, these remained switched on. When I look back, today, I strongly feel-

"Unrestricted free supply of anything will definitely result in wastage; trying to impose metering or restrictions will have to observe a lot of resistance; but, you can get efficiency and better management only after willful metering."

# SuperCalender Production Increase

After coating of clay and similar chemicals, the paper is passed through supercalender to impart good smoothness of paper surface. When the plant started, the main bottleneck was the supercalender itself. Coating machine was able to produce more, and the further process of re-winder and sheet cutters were capable to produce more paper. I started discussing the issue with shift operators. My question used to be straight, "Can you run the supercalender at higher speed? What happens if we increase speed?" The usual answers were dependent on paper. If paper gsm was low (light weight paper), the operator said, "Sir, paper gsm is low, so we need to run at slower speed, otherwise paper breakage may occur." In case the paper gsm was higher, they said, "Sir, paper is of higher gsm. To get good gloss (surface finish), we need to operate it at lower speed."

I decided to monitor the process closely. A non-contact proximity sensor was mounted to a roll journal near keyway. This roll rotated by the paper movement. In case the machine is switched off, or the paper is not running on the machine, that roll would not rotate. The signal from the proximity sensor was fed to a digital counter. By altering internal wiring, the reset button of the counter was disabled. Now, all the shift operators were asked to note down the readings at the start and at the end of their shift. Apparently, our target was shifted from production by ton (weight) to production by length of paper.

After around a week, I analyzed the data gathered. The increase in counter reading was normally 60,000 to 70,000 for two operators while it was just 45,000 to 55,000 for the third. I asked him to meet me in my office. When he came, I told him that for joining the mill, he was referred by Mr. XYZ, whom I respect and that was why I appointed him. But, the mill was getting low production in his shift and the management wanted me to fire him. I then showed him the counter readings and how these indicated proving that the production in his shift was always lower.

Next, I told him that after a lot of efforts from my side, the management was agreed to give him extension for 15 days, and if the situation does not improve, we had to take an action against him. He assured me that there shall be no problem from his side in future. Then, I indicated him to be careful that such increase in production should not result in any deterioration in quality, otherwise, I'd be helpless and forced to take action against him.

Within 3-4 days, readings began to touch 80,000 in his shift. Next week, I called another operator out of the remaining two. The whole story was repeated and he also began to respond better. Within a month, there was a very healthy competition between the three. The counter readings began to reach 1,20,000 to 1,40,000 – almost double production. The total investment for the sensor-counter etc. was a little below Rs.2,000.

The proximity sensor and counter exist still in the unit, but I do not check the readings anymore. Nobody else checks those readings in the plant. A healthy competition is still going on amongst the three and they themselves monitor their own performance.

# Alum Dosing in Machine Chest

To maintain water repellency in paper, rosin and alum were being used long back. Now, another chemical AKD is being used. The aim for rosin is to impart water repellency while alum is used to maintain correct pH of the pulp stock for proper functioning of rosin.

The rosin was added to the pulp in the blending chest, where different pulps (if required) were mixed to maintain different properties of paper. In the next chest, machine chest, alum was being added. Alum comes in solid brick shaped form, each weighing around 18-20 kg. The approach used was to put alum in a tank, where it was being mixed with water. The operator used to put several buckets of this alum solution in the machine chest. For the sake of simplicity, the operators started to use a time based system, like adding 3 buckets of alum solution after every half an hour or so. There was no problem with quality, paper machine runnability or anything with that.

Occasionally, the paper machine runnability got disturbed and they accused of operators for forgetting alum addition at a time, and later too much addition of alum to compensate for the problem. Slowly and slowly, the practice started to increase. The paper machine people, whenever the machine was disturbed, asked the laboratory chemist to check for pH of machine back water, which was on a higher side indicating little or no alum addition. After some time, when checked, they found pH on the lower side. This continued for long, and the machine operators and pulp mill operators were generally seen fighting claiming fault at other end.

One day, a strange idea popped up in mind. The disturbed pH was disturbing the machine or the disturbed machine resulted in pH disturbance. Initially, I tried to shrug off the idea, but after frequent problems, thought over it seriously. In case of every problem, the pulp mill operators indicated that pH in the machine chest was ok.

Later it was observed that the paper machine people increased the paper machine felt shower water pressure for better felt cleaning whenever the machine got disturbed. This way, the whole process water balance got disturbed. Further, disbelieving the pulp mill people, the habit started in paper machine people to add some alum themselves in the pulp in paper machine area. The matter was discussed in detail with the machine people along with some modifications in pipelines to ensure the process is not much affected by the increased water flow in showers.

After this the same problem never appeared again. This indicated that we need to trust operators. An operator may be careless occasionally, but if you are facing frequent problems which appear due to operator carelessness, it is the time to look for other possible reasons behind it.

# MG Bearing Housing Bolt broken

The paper machine uses a huge drying cylinder called as MG. The MG word is abbreviated from Machine Glazed, meaning the paper is glazed at one side. One day, due to breakage of a bolt, both press rolls and two paper machine felts got damaged. In the press section, paper is sandwiched between to felts (blankets) and pressed at high pressure to remove moisture. To further press the paper so that the drying costs are reduced and machine can run at maximum production rate, there are two touch rolls that force the MG cylinder upwards and thus paper is again pressed between these nips. The weight of MG is in the tune of 35-40 MT, and the same is mounted on bearing housing at both ends. Each of the bearing housings has four bolts.

This way, one can see that the weight of MG works in downwards direction, while the touch rolls force the MG upwards. Net resultant force is not very high, though in upwards direction. Even if the upwards force is not much, it must be distributed on eight bolts, so each bolt had to bear only 12.5% load only. Bolts were definitely much stronger than that. Further to add, the bolts were also of a good brand, so there was nothing doubtful about the quality of the bolts.

The plant was stopped immediately after the accident, but, instead of initiating further work, we spent nearly two hours gathering information and possible reasons of the problem. All three remaining bolts of this side were in place, and all the four bolts of opposite side were ok. The bolt was broken from nearly 2" away from head. That meant before striking the press rolls and felts; the top end of the bolt must have popped up with a great force.

We found the bolt in pieces; the nut, one side washer, but the other side spring washer could not be found. We decided to mount new rolls, new felts with caution as the missing spring washer might be lying somewhere in the machine and if it falls on the felts, damage may take place again.

Replacement of rolls, felts meant nearly 20-22 hours shut, and the work was going on with full swing. Meanwhile, I went to my office to transfer photographs taken from mobile to computer, and think what could be the source of the problem. After a few minutes, a shift fitter came to meet me. He seemed a little frightened. He told me with low voice that the spring washer I was searching was not mounted at all. In fact, he himself had gone to fix the bolts around four months back, and the spring washer fell down on ground, and could not be found. That day, he was too tired and ignored the importance of the washer, and hence, as a precaution tightened the bolt fully. He did not tell about it to maintenance In-charge thinking that he would be very annoyed with him. But, after the accident, he felt guilty for the accident so came directly to me to confess.

I too felt very annoyed, but asked him to not discuss the issue with anyone. I further instructed him to go and do his duty so that the machine can be re-started soon, and then after the plant starts, take a leave for a couple of days. Then he should come to me before resuming his duties.

Next day, I discussed the issue with maintenance in-charge. I explained him about the details, possible causes, and the fitter's mindset. Had he informed the in-charge that very day, the problem could have averted. Mistakes do happen by a person doing job. According to me, that major loss was not due to breaking of the bolt or lack of spring washer, but due to the fact that the fitter was afraid that he'd be scolded for negligence. A couple of days later, the fitter was allowed to resume the duties.

For those, with mechanical background, the main suspense still remains why did the bolt break? In fact, a bolt elongates slightly on application of tension. The elongation is proportional to the applied load. To ensure the load on each bolt remains same, all bolts are applied with equal tension while tightening the bolts. Use of spring washer is especially useful, as when a bolt stretches due to excess tension, the spring washer absorbs some of the elongation and thus the load is shifted to other bolts. It is also necessary that the load on all of the bolts do not vary significantly. You might have noticed that when the bolts of car tyre are tightened or loosened, the job is done by screwing or unscrewing all the bolts in different small steps. To further support the equal distribution of load, spring washers are used. In case a bolt elongates due to load, this results in spring washer compression and hence load is shifted to other bolts. This way, no single bolt bears excess load.

In this case, there was no spring washer, and further the bolt was over-tightened. As a result, this single bolt had to bear the entire load. It could not bear the load, so the mills had to bear a loss of more than one million rupees.

However, as the reason was now available and known to all, we can be sure that this event would not get repeated again. Now, we have checked the nut & bolts at other locations also if they might fail due to similar reason, and taken appropriate actions. Have you?

# DC Motor Load Hunting

The paper machine was being run by a DC motor. The objective of DC motor and panel was to ensure constant desired speed of the same. The DC panel indicated two major parameters- voltage and current. DC motor speed is proportional to voltage output of the panel and the current indicated the load on the DC motor.

One evening, the current fluctuation started. Against the normal current of 220 amperes, the same fluctuated between 180 to 270 amperes. The fluctuation in voltage was small, but it was enough to alter the speed of the machine and hence the paper being made was of fluctuating gsm (gram weight per square meter).

Initially, we called the panel supplier, who suggested adjusting some small potentiometers marked as P4, P7, or P11 on the control card in the control panel. To a certain extent, this helped. What seemed odd was that in case of any problem, we needed to first turn P4 clockwise, if problem does not solve, then anticlockwise. In case problem remains the same, try the same with P7 and then P11. There was no standard setting sequence or procedure. Just turn the pot and see what works best for you.

Slowly and slowly, the problem started becoming frequent. Another noticeable point was that the problem usually appeared in the evening. We asked an electrical consultant to look into the problem, but he could not indicate anything proper. He went back saying that there could be something in the stars (astrology).

The mill was facing more and more problems due to this, and suddenly, a DG operator indicated that the problem starts after some time when the diesel is filled in the service tanks. He further indicated that during routine service (after each 300 hours of DG operation), they change the fuel filters, and the fuel filters are being found badly choked, which was not the case earlier.

Now, everything was clear. The 'stars' were really bad. The mill, due to financial constraints, was unable to procure full tanker of diesel from the Government owned depots, so it was procuring diesel from a local petrol pump. Most probably, the diesel was adulterated. All the diesel service tanks were emptied out and found a lot of dirt and rejects in it. It was decided to procure the full tankers directly from depots, and the problem vanished fully.

This electrical problem, that caused a big loss to the mills along with keeping the electrical equipment under threat for a long time was being originated from the poor quality of fuel.

# Bearing Scheduled Maintenance

A plant has a lot of bearings, and in case of any problem related to improper mounting, lubrication, misalignment etc., the failure is a must. The failure cost to the mills is not only the cost of bearing itself, but also includes the cost of bearing sleeve, cost of downtime, and the cost of occasional damage to the roll journal. So, one thing is certain- ensuring minimum downtime due to bearings must be avoided at any cost.

Once, the bearing problem started to increase. Every bearing failure in the paper machine results in a downtime to one to three hours. There were 3-4 such failures in a month. It was decided to make a schedule to open the bearing housing covers and physically check all the bearings after a three months interval. It was also decided to have a planned shut for this in case downtime for some other reason is not available.

The results were bad. In the first shut itself, several bearings were found defective, so these were replaced with new bearings. The plant was started, but, problem remained the same. Rather, the problem increased. Now, the problem originated with recently mounted new bearings. Anyway, the scheme continued for three cycles, and finally dropped after that.

Meanwhile, discussions with bearing experts were going on. Persons inclined towards a particular make or brand of bearing, suggested using that particular brand. Someone suggested considering use of different grade of grease and so and so forth.

As indicated separately in this book, I posted about the problem on 'PaperTechnology' group created to discuss such problems. Next day, a friend in the group messaged me that for the problem, I should talk to Mr. Natha, who is the maintenance head at a paper mill where is worked some time back. I took his number and called Mr. Natha. I told him that the problem is mainly in felt rolls. Mr. Natha asked if the problem was in all rolls or in a few rolls only. I informed that the problem was in few rolls. Then he asked, "Is it true that in some rolls the problem is at operating side bearings while in some other rolls, the problem is at drive side?" Oh yes. It was true. We never thought of this. He then asked, "As a practice, the one side of bearing is kept fixed on bearing housing, while the other side, a little play is left so that the bearing can move to and fro by 2-4 mm. Are your floating bearings the ones which are facing more problems?" Again, he was right. He suggested identifying and locking the bearing which were facing problem.

We did the same, and problem just vanished. After around a month, I called him to say thanks for helping me solve the problem. Then he suggested another point. Not only technical factors are important, you need to ensure that the fitter does not fit the bearing carelessly. In case you find a bearing problem repeating in any of these bearing within 1-2 months, just be present at the machine floor, and ask the fitter about why could the bearing might have failed. Take a couple of photographs of the failed bearing, bearing sleeve, lock nut and lock washer etc. at different angles. The fitter will definitely take enough precaution and you would be surprised by the results.

It happened two or three times, when there were repeated problems, and just my presence during the night shift, my enquiries about the problem, taking a few photographs helped me. Probably the shift fitters thought I was going to discuss the matter with the maintenance head the next day. In a particular case, there were 5 bearing failures during two weeks at a single location. I asked one of the process operators that in case of any repetition of this bearing failure, just call me secretly. The shift maintenance team was busy in replacing the bearing as usual, and they had not called the maintenance head considering it a routine job. But, my presence made them working with a caution, and after that bearing was mounted, there was no problem in that bearing for the next 8 months.

# Digester Safety

While I was a student, I decided to have some additional practical experience. I visited a paper mill nearby and requested them to allow me to visit the mills for 10-15 days. They allowed me. It was an agro based mill, in which the straws, old gunny bags etc. were being cooked in digester. The digester is a huge (4.2 meter diameter ball shaped) pressure vessel, in which the raw material is cooked by pressurized steam and caustic soda to make it soft so that individual fibers can be separated easily in subsequent operations. Steam pressure is critical as the higher the pressure is, the fibers would be easier to separate, however, the yield decreases with more steam pressure. Also several paper strength properties depend on pressure and time inside the digester.

To know what the steam pressure was inside the digester, I reached to the pressure gauge. A lot of dust and old pulp was deposited on the dial, so I removed that with my hand. After cleaning that, I found that the needle of the dial gauge was misplaced, and fallen on the bottom of dial. I turned back. Suddenly an old operator (probably the digester operator) appeared. He was too old to stand straight. He said, *"Bada Saab bolta hai ki pressure 4 kg se jyada nahi jana chahiye. 6 kg chalata hun, guaranty hai jo phat jaye* (Senior Director has asked to maintain a maximum of 4 bar (or kg/cm2) pressure in the digester. I operate at 6 bar and guaranty that it will not blast.)" I thought he has no guaranty of even himself, but is taking responsibility of the digester. It was a funny, but dangerous and very serious issue.

I immediately went to the director office, where his son (son of *bada saab*, he was also one of the directors) was there. I discussed the whole issue to him and requested to take appropriate action in time. He smiled, and said, "My father likes that operator very much as he is one of the oldest employees of the mills. So, we cannot take any action against him. However, I already know about the situation, and as a precaution, have installed a PRV (pressure reducing valve) set at 4.2 bar pressure at the inlet line to the digester. Further, with the help of instrument people, I have set the display to show 6 bar pressure in place of actual pressure. Now, I know the pressure cannot exceed 4.2 bar, and he (the operator) is happy that he is maintaining a higher pressure even against my father's orders."

# Corrupt Vs. Honest

This question was asked during the interaction with seniors when I joined engineering college. The question was, "Out of two persons, one corrupt and one honest, whom would you like to choose?" As obvious, I favored the honest one. Then I was told a story– a real story.

In that hostel, there were around 120-150 students. For students, there was a mess with a good kitchen, dining hall and beautiful furniture. The material like vegetables, flour, spices etc. were procured daily from the local market, and the total purchase amount was equally divided between the students. The salaries of the mess staff were being paid directly by the university.

To keep an eye on the expenses, every year, the students elected fiver persons amongst them – one CMC (Chief Mess Councilor) and four MC (Mess Councilors). The average mess bill remained Rs. 330-350 per month those days. Elections took place, and a new team took its position. The CMC woke up early next morning, and went to the wholesale vegetable market at 4:00AM. In the wholesale market, if you reach early, you can get good bargains, and better quality. He just watched the business going on there, and collected information on the prevailing rates. This continued for next two days. All the remaining MCs were doing their jobs as usual- nothing special about them. The fourth day, he called the mess servant going to procure potato from a shop and asked him to procure the same from another shop. Yes, the price was 40% less here. Similar action was taken for other vegetables also.

But, a student cannot go to vegetable market daily. He needs time for studies also. So he asked the mess servant to buy at specified price range only. In case he finds that the prices of capsicum are higher, as an alternate he could buy lady finger. So another weekly menu was prepared indicating the alternate vegetables etc. In case the vegetable indicated in the main menu was not available, the alternate vegetable could be purchased.

As a next step, he started looking into the cooking process. He spent time with cook, and observed some cooking practices. He noted down these in detail, and called his mother to know if some saving was possible in existing method. She gave a few tips, and that resulted in reduced spices consumption as well as reduced fuel consumption also.

He knew that the food bill for the next month was going to be lesser. In the mess, some of the items were given to students in limited quantity- for example, during breakfast, any number of breads, but 20 gm butter and one glass of milk. However, if any student wished, he could have taken such items as extra and the price of that item had to be added in his monthly bill. But, one morning, he called the mess servant, and ordered him to bring him another piece of butter and a glass of milk, but not charge the extra amount in his bill. Obviously, the extra consumption had to be paid by all students.

A couple of students resisted slightly, but during breakfast, everyone is in a hurry to go to attend the classes, so the matter suppressed. But the same thing happened next day also. Incidentally, it was a Sunday. Anyway, some students decided not to raise the issue in the mess itself to maintain the decorum and discuss the issue in the hostel. A meeting was called and all students, except the mess council were asked to attend the same. It was decided that the CMC had been charged with corruption and being a co-student, should be given opportunity to resign from the post. If he disagreed, all students would go to hostel warden and request him to sack the CMC and call for re-election.

Next, four MCs were called and asked if they were with students or want to go with CMC. Obviously, they decided to support the student's decision. Now, CMC was called up. A student briefed him up the whole issue and the decision made by the students.

It was CMC turn now. He flatly told that the mess bill which had been in the range of Rs. 330-350 a month for the past several months; was going to be less than Rs. 240 that month. That could have been made possible by the vigilant steps taken by him. He further explained that going to wholesale vegetable market just to cross check and verify the rates at which the things were procured needs some time, some effort. Going to vegetable market nearly four to five kilometers away on his bicycle almost once or twice every week was not an easy job.

He, later, turned to MCs –the members of his team- and asked them if they had, even once, visited the vegetable market? Have they asked why the breads were being procured at MRP (retail price) while the requirement was in bulk? Were they acting as MCs or just as accountant to see the calculation mistakes in different bills only? He then, took a paper, nicely folded, from the pocket of his shirt and said that he was going to resign if any one, - even a single student- wanted so. But whoever becomes new CMC must assure and be ready to maintain mess bill around what has already been achieved. He further indicated that he wanted those extra items as a token of acceptance of his extra work.

Needless to say, he continued his term, and got elected next year also- unopposed.

In today's time, honesty vs. corruption debate has gone so far away, that the people have started ignoring the level of basic quality of our elected members- "How result oriented are they?"

# Spelling of Ball

To get pure milk without any adulteration, long back I used to go to a nearby village daily to get milk for home. I got milk from a small family of husband, wife and a small school going kid. There were two cows with them. One day, when I reached there, the boy was doing his home work speaking the spelling of ball as B-O-L-L-Ball. I looked at his notebook. The teacher had written the same word 'B-O-L-L" four times in the header line, and the students had to rewrite it on the full page and cram the spelling. Not only this, the symbol of the ball was also drawn on top of the page. I corrected the word as BALL and told that the correct word is ball, not boll. By this time, milk was ready, and I returned back.

Next day, when I reached there, the father of boy was sitting angry. With his a big wooden stick was kept by the side, as if he was willing to beat me with that. He almost shouted on me, "What did you tell to my son? His teacher gave him two tight slaps." I felt stunned. I took my mobile, and starting the dictionary app, tried to show him the correct word. But, he was not ready to listen anything. For a moment I thought that I should go to the teacher and explain him the correct word, but, I was afraid that the teacher might get convinced with me for the time being, but may punish more that child again just to take revenge. Anyway, though with difficulty, I was able to convince the father that what I told was ok, but he decided that the son should learn only what his teacher says.

For a couple of days, I felt very guilty. I wanted to do something, but could not decide what to do.

Later in 2104, our honorable PM, during the Independence Day speech urged the educated ones to teach students in rural areas – free of cost-, at least once in every week or month or whatever seem suitable to them. I liked the idea and started thinking to move ahead. But a question appeared in my mind- which school? Should I start it in a private school, where they charge more fees from the students, and pay less to teachers? Or should I begin with the government schools where the teachers are well paid, but infrastructural facilities are not there? It was a difficult decision. However, I contacted a couple of private schools to initiate with a guest lecture. But, they did not show any interest. I thought of going to some Government funded school, but hesitated as they might not like me to teach there. After spending a lot of time in confusion, I just dropped the idea.

It is common for the little students to trust more to their teachers. That way, the responsibility of a teacher is greatly enhanced.

Considering the overall scenario, one can understand that a good management can achieve much better results even with lower salaried staff; rather than with highly paid staff using poor management practices.

# Delivery Issues

We needed a centrifugal pump for the paper machine. Earlier, we were using pumps manufactured from a local supplier. This time, we decided to try a branded pump from a reputed supplier. We sent enquiry by email and post, but no reply appeared.

Then we came to know about a small dealer who was supplying the pump from same manufacturer and claiming to be the authorized dealer. Anyway, we ordered a pump. The performance was very good. During next few years, we procured several pumps for different applications from him and were almost satisfied with the same.

Now, we needed a pump for thermic fluid heater. We asked them to quote, finalized the prices and discount and placed the order. The scheduled delivery was 6 weeks. After 4 weeks, I just called the supplier, and he assured that the pump was under process and was expected to be ready within time. Fifth and sixth week passed, but there was no response from the supplier. Every time, we go the reply that the pump was expected next week. Slowly and slowly, 4 months passed.

I tried to search the manufacturer contact details from internet, and called him directly. This time, I was told that the pump was even not under process as the order was not accepted by the manufacturer. On calling the supplier, he informed that there was some payment issue pending between the two –the supplier and the manufacturer- since long. The manufacturer refused to deliver any pump before the accounts are squared up. Now, this was a purely clear battle between the manufacturer and supplier and the customer was suffering.

Next day, I wrote email to every email id I could find related to the manufacturer about my case. A junior management executive sent me a private message giving the contact details of their VP and requested me not to disclose his name. In fact, he did not tell me his name. All he wanted was a satisfied customer or his company and to ensure that the existing customers do not leave the company for the stupid faults of middle management. I'd like to wish him all the best in his life. In today's times, it is extremely difficult to find such employees who care for their company with such passion and selflessly.

Immediately, I called the VP and explained him the whole situation. He flatly refused that as per company policy, they accept orders through dealers/suppliers, and not from customers. I offered him to pay full payment in advance, but I must get the pump definitely within one month. He might, if he wish pay the dealer commission directly to him. Anyway, he refused quoting their company policy.

It was a bad situation for me. The customer is happy with the performance, manufacturing, workmanship, quality, price, but for silly transaction disputes with their dealer, they were not supplying the material. I called at landline number of the person who gave me VP's contact details, but that number was of some PCO. That well wisher did not want to disclose his name.

Somehow, I managed to get the contact details of the manufacturer's dealer working in some other city, and he agreed to deliver the pump to me within reasonable time. Later, I asked this new dealer why the delivery was so late. Can they not make it faster? He said that the pumps are made against specific requirements from customer, and hence it takes a lot of time. I indicated that the pump I needed was the feed pump generally used in a conventional thermic fluid heater of a capacity of 10 L kCal/hr. At present more than 10000 such installations are there in India. If you try to maintain such inventory, and the customer needs a slightly smaller pump this pump can be offered for a customer who is in a hurry. But he said that the manufacturer does not want to maintain any inventory. Anyway, he agreed to keep an inventory of that pump for me, just for no additional price.

In many cases, consumer is most unhappy with the poor marketing policies. Companies do a lot of work to improve quality, workmanship, performance etc., but there have been instances that the order goes to some other supplier because of poor marketing response.

# Sizing of Paper

Water repellency is an important property of paper. Have you noticed that it is difficult to write on a blotting paper using a fountain pen? If paper absorbs ink too quickly, it is difficult to write or even print on paper. This property is measured by Cobb test. In this test, paper is subjected to water for 60 seconds, and the weight of water absorbed per unit area of paper is measured in grams per square meter (gsm) is defined as Cobb value. Most consumers demand that the Cobb value should be less than say 20 or 25 or something for the paper they procure. A high Cobb value means paper can absorb more water.

For a particular grade of paper, the consumers were, however, unaware of the testing methodologies. Whenever they faced a problem, they just said that the paper is taking (absorbing) too much water. A mill decided to standardize its operations and it was decided that the mill shall maintain a Cobb value of less than 45 for that grade of paper. To maintain the desired Cobb value, gum (Gum Rosin) and alum were being added in paper. The rosin consumption was almost 15-20 kg/Ton of paper. The more was rosin addition, the more was water repellency in paper.

After some time, a customer complained of more water absorption by paper. The mill checked its records and found that the Cobb was maintained between 40 and 45, as decided earlier. It was further decided that the Cobb target should be reduced to 35-40 for future supplies. There was a little increase in rosin consumption, but the customer complaint vanished. Again after a couple of months, the same complaint appeared. This time, considering that it was a rainy season, hence, the paper is absorbing more and more moisture and hence the problem was appearing, so the target Cobb was further reduced.

Again the same thing happened after 6 months. After every problem, the mill looked at past 2-3 months figures, and finding everything under control, decided to reduce Cobb standard, thinking that they are improving quality. This however, was cutting the pockets of the mills. The rosin consumption increased to 70 kg/Ton of paper. The cob target now was less than 20. Again the same complaint appeared.

A computer savvy quality control manager from the mill spent a lot of time, and made a beautiful plot of month wise average Cobb value for all hourly Cobb testing results available for past year. He further collected that month wise specific rosin consumption (rosin per ton of paper) data, and plotted these on a graph paper. The graph was presented in the next quality meeting and he requested to investigate the matter further. The marketing manager, who was attending this meeting for the first time, indicated that he had himself investigated the matter and found that whenever a new operator joined with that consumer, he raised such complaint. Instead of reducing Cobb, giving the consumer an assurance that we have taken his complaint seriously and he will not face such problem in future, is all that was enough for that consumer.

On a trial basis, in the next lot, the Cobb target was increased to 35-40, and the paper was sent to the same consumer. There was no complaint this time. Rosin consumption decreased from 70 to 30-35 kg per ton of paper.

Focusing on quality is always a good approach, but at times when the companies start becoming too fanatic towards quality it may result in more problems.

# When Quality Poses Risk

A well known and highly reputed paper mill was making only specialty grade paper. The paper, that that time was being supplied to a very popular biscuit maker as an interleaf between the product and packaging. It was something like butter paper, with a translucent look. The paper mill was said to have the monopoly to produce that grade.

As told by some of the technology experts, the cost of production by the mill that time was Rs.34-36 a kg, while it could have been reduced to Rs.24-26 a kg just by taking few simple steps towards cost cutting. The mill was selling this product at a cost of Rs.60 a kg, and hence did not make any effort to reduce the cost of production. The mill, in fact, was enjoying its USP of making that grade of paper.

A few years later, another reputed mill tried to capture this good business opportunity with that grade of paper and started R&D to develop that grade of paper. Meanwhile, to understand the requirements they contacted the biscuit supplier also and made several visits to biscuit manufacturer. This message spread like hot news in the existing mills, which became cautious but still did not initiate their efforts towards cost cutting or development of other grades of paper. Anyway, their trials failed, and they withdrew from R&D trials for making this paper.

The earlier paper mill, overwhelmed with the news, decided to increase the product prices. Now, they were the undisputed leader and sole supplier for that particular grade of paper, and knew that no paper mill in India could pose any risk to their business. They decided to increase the prices. The increase was significant –from Rs. 60 a kg earlier to Rs.70 a kg.

Meanwhile, the biscuit supplier's business was spreading and R&D was also going on in their laboratories to find some alternate to this supplier. Working with a monopoly vendor has its own risks. If something happens to that vendor, your business affects badly. So they decided to try PP (Polypropylene) for packing of the biscuits. PP worked well, and the quality of biscuits remained better in PP packaging. The printing results were also drastically better. Moreover, the packaging cost with PP was just 50-60% compared to the earlier packaging –paper. Still, the biscuit supplier had to decide whether to maintain the old tradition of packaging or go with a new packaging.

The meeting was going on at the biscuit supplier office to evaluate the pros and cons of PP packaging compared to the existing conventional packaging, while they received the intimation of price hike. Within moments, the meeting turned in favor of PP, and the paper mill lost its business from virtually the sole consumer.

The paper mill, later tried to make other grades of paper, but as their whole process was too deficient, they could not sustain in the market. Within a couple of months, this mill had to shut permanently.

After the mill was shut, I got a chance to visit the mills. I noticed two large stainless steel storage chests each around 25-30 kiloliter capacity, just near to paper machine section. Confused, why such stainless storage chests were there, I asked a person passing by, "What for these chests have been provided?" He informed that those chests were for storing milk. I was more confused now. What for the milk was being used for making paper? On asking, his reply was, "Because they were making milky paper- Paper, white as milk" Of course, we use optical brightening agents to make paper look brighter, but use of milk was something stupid. Anyway, the infrastructure looked like a big mill, and more surprising was that fact that the mill was making just 10%-20% of paper, compared to similar machines installed in other mills.

If the production unit starts becoming fanatic over quality, it becomes the need of the time to revaluate over its vision, goals, targets, and manufacturing practices. When I look back today, I can recall five or six paper mills which enjoyed a very good reputation in terms of quality being made. All of these earned good profits also, for several years. But, none of them is running now.

# Worker Demands in Small Villages

While a mill was started in a village, initially, there was the requirement of skilled manpower. Most of the appointments were made, and unskilled manpower was also easily available. When the plant was stabilized, there was practically no need of additional manpower. Thus, there was a no-vacancy situation.

Few weeks later, a local villager contacted me for placement of his son. He wanted the job for his son for any post. I refused, saying that there was no requirement at that time. He insisted a lot, so, reluctantly I asked him to come to me next week, but, he went saying that he would come after three days. He appeared the next day itself. Again, he continued with the same request. Finally, he offered me something. I could appoint his son, without paying anything. If that was not enough, he was ready to pay me the salary for his son, and I need not pay anything to his son for the job. I got confused with the offer. Someone bringing his son for a job and offering you a salary for the placement

I told the production manager the whole story. He smiled and informed that in their (that villager's) community the sex ratio is significantly skewed. Getting a bride for marriage is very difficult. If a boy is having a job, he can get a bride easily. That is why that villager was in desperate need for the job of his son. If you had offered him a job, the boy could be married within a month or so, and left the job. If you hire such people, they do not work to earn monthly salary, but to earn a bride. Then they start looking after their parental farming or whatsoever.

Just a few days later, the production manager asked me not to visit the production floor for a few hours. Some people were coming to the plant to meet a helper (unskilled worker) for the marriage purpose. For that day, the helper sat in shift in-charge chair, and other workers, while he was talking to the bride relatives; passed by wishing him "good morning sir!" Obviously, the visitors were very impressed with the position of that boy, and his marriage was fixed the same day. He left the job within a couple of months.

# Freebies

Who doesn't like freebies? With almost every second product you buy from market, you may get some freebie. But, can the same thing happen with services provided by an individual? Can an individual employee give some freebies to his company?

In a mill located near a small village the initial major problem was availability of workers. At the time where mobile phones were not there, landline phone connectivity was poor, in case of any breakdown in any machinery, calling a welder or electrician was difficult. Shift electrical or mechanical staff used to try their level best, and if they were not able to solve the problem, the routine was to call the head of department. HOD, on reaching the mills, on the basis of the nature of problem, he decided which worker had to be called and the driver was sent again to pick up that person from home.

Mill decided to have a dedicated driver with a car for this purpose. A driver, Nafees' approached for this job. The duty was of 24 hours, he had to stay in factory, and in case of any problem, when the process shift in-charge, shift maintenance fitter or shift electrician called, he had to go to the relevant person's home to call him. A room was made available to him, and he was free to sleep, take rest whenever he was not required to go anywhere for any reason. First few days went on well. There was no problem in the plant, and he just spent his time gossiping or sleeping. Then at one night, there was some mechanical problem, and the shift fitter asked him to bring with him the mechanical head. Instead of going immediately, Nafees did something else, he went inside the machine hall, and asked a worker about what had happened. Obviously, he could not understand the details, but knew something. Then he reached to the mechanical head residence, and pushed the doorbell. When the mechanical head opened the door,

Nafees told him, "There is some problem in the plant, and the machine has stopped. Shift fitter asked me to bring you with me to the factory. Behind the machine near the electrical control room, there is a green tank. They were saying that some jali has been jammed." Now, the mechanical head could understand that the paper machine pressure screen basket had got choked, and it needs to be removed for cleaning. He told Nafees to drop him outside the factory gate and call two fitters from nearby villages.

Next day, the mechanical head narrated the whole case indicating had Nafees not briefed him the case, he would have gone inside the plant, discussed the issue with production people and then decided to call those two workers. That could have resulted in increase of downtime by another 10-15 minutes. A driver is not supposed to have knowledge about the plant and machinery. But, getting the basic information supplied by the workers, he informed the same to mechanical head. This approach by the driver saved 10-15 minutes of downtime.

Needless to say, there are many drivers, but Nafees has earned a special respect out of all.

In another case, almost during the time above; the mill got a new customer from Assam. Sending some product from western UP to Assam was not that easy those times. Most trucks available in the locality had a local permit and could not transport goods to other states of India. A new transporter Sher Singh contacted the mills through some reference. That time, he was having nearly 8-10 trucks, and was considered a reliable person by few other mills. After the negotiations, a couple of days later, the first truck reached the mills. Sher Singh was there with the truck. While the driver was busy in getting the truck weighed, positioning for loading etc., Sher Singh requested to visit inside the production hall. He was allowed for the same. Later, he came to office and asked if he could make an STD call. There were no mobile phones those days, and STD calls were also very costly. I don't remember why, but I allowed. He dialed the number and told someone, *"Bauji, maal to achchha ban raha hai, joint bhi nahi hai. Badhiya mill hai."* (Sir, the product they are making, is good; there are no joints in paper. This is a good mill.). Within an hour or so, we got another phone call from the same consumer in Assam to deliver around four more truckload of the same material, by the same transport only.

Later we came to know that this transporter used to go to the mills, and sent feedback to consumers about the quality of product. That made the consumers sitting far away, more confident about the supplier. Obviously, the consumer as well as the supplier both preferred this transporter over the others.

Whatever your job profile may be, if you are giving something extra to your employer, your work will definitely go noticed, sooner or later. You might have received many freebies, but are you ready to give any to your company or profession?

# Quality of Product or Infrastructure

Often we rate the quality of our products substandard. Have you ever thought why it is so? Who is really responsible for the poor quality of products? Let me share a practical case.

A paper mill produces paper. The paper deckle (width) remains the same, the machine speed is fixed for a particular set of operating conditions, and the paper making pulp enters from a pulp stock chest of uniform quality. After the chest begins to empty, next lot of pulp is transferred to the chest, and the process goes on.

Now, if the two different lots of stock in the chest have different consistency (concentrations), the basis weight of paper (grams per square meter or gsm) will vary. A good operator must check the consistency of each chest of pulp before transferring and do the necessary steps so that the pulp consistency remains the same. To help the operators, now a days, we have good automation including consistency transmitters and controllers, and maintaining the same shall not be a problem.

Still, many mills complain of gsm variation. Yes! I have used the word 'mills' in place of writing just the word 'consumers'. If you look at the process thoroughly, you have maintained the machine speed using VFDs, so the machine speed is really fixed. But several other motors are directly driven by the conventional starters and any variation in supply voltage and frequency results in speed variation in these, and hence the operating parameters alter time to time.

Let us look at the magnitude. Suppose you have installed a voltage stabilizer, still +2% variation is obvious with best voltage stabilizers. Add to this the effect of frequency; that again fluctuates to the tune of +2% or more. As a result, the input flow through pump may change by +4% or so. Now, add to this the machine errors etc. This makes the overall possible error to the tune of +5% or so. When an operator is working in such situations, he obviously, slowly and slowly starts considering these variations as normal and as a result, the quality becomes inferior.

Long back in a paper mill, the electricity supply was met from the DG sets only. The mill was running smooth without major quality issues. Later, when due to increasing HSD prices, DG sets became nonviable, and the mill switched over to grid supply, it was observed that the gsm variations increased. Initially, it was thought that the operators had become careless, but after thorough investigation the root cause could be found out. To certain extent some steps were taken to minimize the problem, but, nobody can deny that getting a world class product needs world class infrastructure also.

In a similar case, we needed to install a supercalender for the upcoming paper coating plant. This equipment included a number of rolls. For better quality of product to be produced we decided that the rolls should be chrome plated and super-finished. Chrome plating a roll having a diameter of around 800mm with a face length of 2300mm and weight nearing 10 ton is not a simple job. The process involved to send the roll to a supplier in one city for grinding and pre-finishing, then to second city for electroplating, then back to first city for final finishing, then back to us. One roll, when reached to chrome plating unit was rejected saying that there was some minor dent on the roll and it had to be grinded again. Next time, when the roll was sent from the chrome plating facility to final super-finishing one, due to poor road, the truck carrying the roll turned upside down, causing major damage to the roll. Now, it was grinded again and sent for chrome plating again. The chrome plating for such a roll needed 48 hours continuous electricity supply, with no discontinuity for more than 30 minutes.

Next day, there was a power cut, and on contacting the state owned electricity department, they assured that the supply will resume within 10-15 minutes. On their assurance, DG was not started (as the chrome plating person was not interested in several switchovers to produce a better quality), but power could resume only after one hour.

The chrome plating expert decided to de-chrome the roll, send it again for grinding and pre-finishing. And do the chrome plating again. We had been fed up by now, and asked him saying that our project had already delayed by five weeks, to return back the roll to us, without chrome plating. He refused saying that it would be against his reputation. We offered him to pay his full chrome plating charges, but he, the proud retired officer of Indian Army refused to accept any money without completing the job. For him, this was not just a business, it was a mission.

Anyway, next week the roll was ready and its performance was excellent. I must agree, at times, we cursed the chrome plating man during the project delay period, yet, today I respect him a lot for his sincerity, ethics and no-compromise nature. He did not charge anything extra, and incurred a big financial loss (nearly double of the roll chrome plating bill), while, we had to pay five times grinding and super-finishing charges extra than required, as well as freight charges nearly 3 times than these should be; in addition to nearly one and a half month delay.

However, the question remains the same- When the whole project is being delayed by 6-7 weeks just for a single piece of equipment is it easy to stick to quality? In most cases, people would choose to compromise, and when you start compromising the first compromise would always be with quality of the product.

# Effluent Testing

A friend running a paper mill called me to assess the operational practices and performance of ETP (Effluent Treatment Plant) installed there. He seemed in urgency, and wanted me to find out if there was something wrong going on there. I reached the next day. When I reached there, we decided to immediately go to ETP posing myself as some Government officer and assess the same.

The ETP operator and the chemist were there and after asking a few questions, I asked the chemist to show me the facilities available in their laboratory. The mill had set up a dedicated beautiful laboratory for effluent testing purpose with all latest testing equipment, and the characteristics of treated effluent, mainly BOD, COD, TSS, TDS and pH were being tested daily.

I asked him to show me the log books, which he showed. The log-books were very neat and clean and all the parameters were well in the limit, for past two months. Apparently, they were maintaining the parameters well. Anyway, I was able to observe something wrong, so I asked him to go outside the lab and wait for five minutes. As he left, I told my friend that everything seems OK, the readings are well, but all the readings are fake.

This was a little shocking for him. He immediately came to the point. A senior Government officer was his friend and he requested this Government officer to visit to his plant in the personal capacity as a friend, and he also used the same words, "All the readings are good, but fake." He wanted me to tell how I was able to come to that conclusion just by looking at the log books. I explained him the whole procedure and reminded about the 'significant figures' and how the readings of different test should meet some basic criteria.

Later, I called the chemist in, and asked him to explain me the test procedure in detail. He started speaking very fast, just to divert my attention. This was again a clear sign of his try to cover his ignorance. He misspelled a reagent name as Magnesium (Mg) Sulphate, which should be correctly used as Manganous (Mn) Sulphate. I asked him to show me the reagent, but the box he showed to me was Magnesium Sulphate. This confirmed that the testing was not being done properly. Next I asked him a few more points, and he admitted that most of the readings were being written without actual testing.

While I was returning back, a question popped up in my mind. I visit the effluent lab in our plant, and can be pretty sure that the chemists are doing actual testing. But, how can a mill owner be sure of these things? The solution appeared as a periodical audit of operational practices audit, by some other mills. This mill, later initiated the same by hiring the chemist from some other nearby mill to make 3-4 visits in his plant and report in case there was any irregularity observed.

Later, different mills joined hands to exchange their effluent samples and cross check the parameters being maintained, so the possibility of any negligence by the chemist is minimized. This further resulted is better cooperation between mills, knowledge sharing on the subject, and finally a better environment.

# Cold Chicken

For the in-plant training during my B.Tech., I visited a broiler farm installed nearby. The farm had several sheds in which chicks (one day old) were put and grown to attain a body weight of nearly 2 kg and finally sold to dealers. These birds take typically 40-50 days to grow to this weight before they are sold. First day, everything was just something new. There were birds of different age in different sheds of 3 days, 12 days, 28 days and 35 days.

I had never imagined of such situation. Nearly 12000-20000 birds in each shed, making noise, running here and there, drinking water from the drinking like or eating feed from the pans. However, I liked the most the instrumentation and automation. Each of the sheds was being controlled by a PLC and the main parameters were temperature, humidity, feed line, drinking line, and lighting. In all, the birds were living in a very comfortable atmosphere.

The system was quite simple. You need to set all the parameters in the PLC control panel, which had a very good UI (User interface) for the whole lot say for 45-50 days. If you need, you may alter set points for different parameters in between; otherwise, there should be no need to interfere with the control system. Of course, the operator, if he wished, may change set points as and when required, or decide to run the whole system in 'manual' mode.

For a couple of days, the farm people considered me an outsider. But soon after they came to know about my IT branch, they started discussing panel related problems. The major problem seemed very funny to me.

The farm manager had no experience of running an automatic shed, and was more comfortable with manual control. He indicated that the temperature was higher than the set point and the computer

(PLC) was not able to lower it down. Well, it was a hot and humid summer time, and the temperature control by running all the ventilating fans and cooler pumps had its own limitations. Cooling pump stopped occasionally due to high humidity condition, and against the set point of 25.1 deg centigrade, the sheds were running at 26.6 deg centigrade. Well, when nature shows its peak, you need to tolerate a little. But the other problem was something else.

According to him, the birds were feeling cold. The birds were sitting in form of different flocks. He told that the birds sitting in that way meant that the birds were feeling cold. Now, this was a tough situation for me. The same man, in the same shed says that the temperature is more than desired one, but he is also saying that the birds were feeling cold. I could not say anything.

That night, I spent a lot of time on internet, and found that the wind results in evaporation from the body. As a result, under the flow of air, one feels lower temperature than it actually is. On searching the PLC supplier's documentation, the same point was indicated there.

I explained him the whole process and control theory, and showed how to compensate the effect of wind in the system. They adjusted the set points accordingly, and reportedly felt much better than earlier.

I feel this was originally the fault of the PLC supplier. Had he given proper training and concepts implemented in developing the system, the operators could have been more comfortable to use these.

# About the Authors

**D K Singhal**

deveshksinghal@gmail.com

D K Singhal is a well known name in Indian Paper Industry. He has nearly 100 publications of research and technical nature to his credit. He did B.E. & M.E. (Pulp & Paper) from University of Rorkee (Now, IIT Roorkee) in 1990 and 1993 respectively. He is Certified Energy Auditor, Chartered Engineer also. He is also the Editorial Adviser to IPPTA (Indian Pulp & Paper Technical Association).

**Dhawal Singhal**

dhawal.singhal@outlook.com

Dhawal Singhal is a B.Tech. (Information Technology) from Manipal University. He is presently working with SapientNitro. He has two publications to his credit.